THE
HISTORY
OF
ISSUES

Censorship

Other Books in the History of Issues series:

THE
HISTORY
OF
ISSUES

Censorship

Kate Burns, Book Editor

GREENHAVEN PRESS

An imprint of Thomson Gale, a part of The Thomson Corporation

THOMSON

™

GALE

Detroit • New York • San Francisco • New Haven, Conn. • Waterville, Maine • London

Christine Nasso, *Publisher*
Elizabeth Des Chenes, *Managing Editor*

© 2007 Thomson Gale, a part of The Thomson Corporation.

Thomson and Star logo are trademarks and Gale and Greenhaven Press are registered trademarks used herein under license.

For more information, contact:
Greenhaven Press
27500 Drake Rd.
Farmington Hills, MI 48331-3535
Or you can visit our Internet site at http://www.gale.com

ISBN 13: 978-0-7377-2009-9
ISBN 10: 0-7377-2009-3

Library of Congress Control Number: 2006935864

Printed in the United States of America
10 9 8 7 6 5 4 3 2 1

Contents

Foreword

In the 1940s, at the height of the Holocaust, Jews struggled to create a nation of their own in Palestine, a region of the Middle East that at the time was controlled by Britain. The British had placed limits on Jewish immigration to Palestine, hampering efforts to provide refuge to Jews fleeing the Holocaust. In response to this and other British policies, an underground Jewish resistance group called Irgun began carrying out terrorist attacks against British targets in Palestine, including immigration, intelligence, and police offices. Most famously, the group bombed the King David Hotel in Jerusalem, the site of a British military headquarters. Although the British were warned well in advance of the attack, they failed to evacuate the building. As a result, ninety-one people were killed (including fifteen Jews) and forty-five were injured.

Early in the twentieth century, Ireland, which had long been under British rule, was split into two countries. The south, populated mostly by Catholics, eventually achieved independence and became the Republic of Ireland. Northern Ireland, mostly Protestant, remained under British control. Catholics in both the north and south opposed British control of the north, and the Irish Republican Army (IRA) sought unification of Ireland as an independent nation. In 1969, the IRA split into two factions. A new radical wing, the Provisional IRA, was created and soon undertook numerous terrorist bombings and killings throughout Northern Ireland, the Republic of Ireland, and even in England. One of its most notorious attacks was the 1974 bombing of a Birmingham, England, bar that killed nineteen people.

In the mid-1990s, an Islamic terrorist group called al Qaeda began carrying out terrorist attacks against American targets overseas. In communications to the media, the organization listed several complaints against the United States. It generally opposed all U.S. involvement and presence in the Middle East. It particularly objected to the presence of U.S. troops in Saudi Arabia, which is the home of several Islamic holy sites. And it strongly condemned the United States for supporting the nation of Israel, which it claimed was an oppressor of Muslims. In 1998 al Qaeda's leaders issued a fatwa (a religious legal statement) calling for Muslims to kill Americans. Al Qaeda acted on this order many times—most memorably on September 11, 2001, when it attacked the World Trade Center and the Pentagon, killing nearly three thousand people.

These three groups—Irgun, the Provisional IRA, and al Qaeda—have achieved varied results. Irgun's terror campaign contributed to Britain's decision to pull out of Palestine and to support the creation of Israel in 1948. The Provisional IRA's tactics kept pressure on the British, but they also alienated many would-be supporters of independence for Northern Ireland. Al Qaeda's attacks provoked a strong U.S. military response but did not lessen America's involvement in the Middle East nor weaken its support of Israel. Despite these different results, the means and goals of these groups were similar. Although they emerged in different parts of the world during different eras and in support of different causes, all three had one thing in common: They all used clandestine violence to undermine a government they deemed oppressive or illegitimate.

The destruction of oppressive governments is not the only goal of terrorism. For example, terror is also used to minimize dissent in totalitarian regimes and to promote extreme ideologies. However, throughout history the motivations of terrorists have been remarkably similar, proving the old adage that "the more things change, the more they remain the same." Arguments for and against terrorism thus boil down to the same set of universal arguments regardless of the age: Some argue that terrorism is justified to change (or, in the case of state terror, to maintain) the prevailing political order; others respond that terrorism is inhumane and unacceptable under any circumstances. These basic views transcend time and place.

Similar fundamental arguments apply to other controversial social issues. For instance, arguments over the death penalty have always featured competing views of justice. Scholars cite biblical texts to claim that a person who takes a life must forfeit his or her life, while others cite religious doctrine to support their view that only God can take a human life. These arguments have remained essentially the same throughout the centuries. Likewise, the debate over euthanasia has persisted throughout the history of Western civilization. Supporters argue that it is compassionate to end the suffering of the dying by hastening their impending death; opponents insist that it is society's duty to make the dying as comfortable as possible as death takes its natural course.

Greenhaven Press's The History of Issues series illustrates this constancy of arguments surrounding major social issues. Each volume in the series focuses on one issue—including terrorism, the death penalty, and euthanasia—and examines how the debates have both evolved and remained essentially the same over the years. Primary documents such as newspaper articles, speeches, and government reports illuminate historical developments and offer perspectives from throughout history. Secondary sources provide overviews and commentaries from a more contemporary perspective. An introduction begins each anthology and supplies essential context and background. An annotated table of contents, chronology, and index allow for easy reference, and a bibliography and list of organizations to contact point to additional sources of information on the book's topic. With these features, The History of Issues series permits readers to glimpse both the historical and contemporary dimensions of humanity's most pressing and controversial social issues.

Introduction

Censorship is the suppression of any speech or material that is considered objectionable or harmful. There are many motivations for this practice. Some censors desire to ban the broadcast or publication of information and images out of a fear that certain forms of expression can be dangerous. For example, those who seek to limit the amount of violence shown on prime-time television worry that young viewers exposed to gratuitous acts of hatred—including murder, rape, and abuse—will come to believe that brutality is an acceptable and even venerated solution to conflict. Other people wish to censor various publications because of their conviction that certain moral or religious beliefs should not be challenged or lampooned in so-called respectable society. Illustrating this position, in September 2005 several Muslim leaders in the Middle East condemned several European newspapers for publishing cartoons that presented caricatures of the Muslim prophet Muhammad. Iranian president Mahmoud Ahmadinejad canceled trade contracts with countries that published the cartoons, and a top leader of the Palestinian Hamas party declared that the cartoonist should be punished by death. On the other hand, many around the world defended the publishers' right to free speech and argued that since the newspapers frequently printed cartoons poking fun at other religions, they were not singling out Muslims for attack. Finally, still other censors seek to limit access to classified information in order to preserve national safety. President Franklin D. Roosevelt created the Office of Censorship during World War II for this reason. The office worked to make sure that the American media did not report any information that could be of value to the enemy.

Whether driven to protect children, ensure national security, prevent moral decay, or suppress rebellion, censorship aims to restrict the distribution of specified information. The degree to which it is successful often depends on the power of the person or group enforcing the regulations. However, even imposing governments, religious organizations, and cultural institutions often have great difficulty in regulating communication and restricting information. In quite a few instances, the suppression of a newspaper article, painting, government report, or movie has backfired because once material becomes prohibited, more people than ever before seem to become curious about it. As Roman historian Tacitus wisely stated, "Things forbidden have a secret charm."

One example of the way in which censorship can lead to greater public interest in the banned subject is the case of Mae West, a vaudeville actress during the 1920s. She fell under the suspicion of New York City officials who objected to her provocative dress and sexual banter during her performances. In 1927 police officers raided the theater where she was acting in her Broadway show *Sex* and arrested her for "corrupting the morals of the youth." Yet the incident ultimately benefited West because the publicity she received from her ten-day jail sentence gave her nationwide exposure and helped her achieve stardom. As West later remarked, "I believe in censorship . . . I made a fortune out of it."

Another unintended affect of censorship is that it can encourage the banned forms of expression to flourish because it sometimes inspires those who have been restricted to be even more creative in their efforts to express their ideas. Again, Mae West's battle over censorship provides a strong example of the way censorship can backfire. Later in her career, when she continued to challenge the mores of sexual decorum in the new Hollywood talkies of the 1930s, the powerful "Hays Office" censored the content of her films. The Motion Picture Producers and Distributors Association, headed by Will H. Hays, required that all American movies conform to a detailed list of regulations called the "Production Code." When censors watched West's films, scenes featuring her bawdy jokes and suggestive dancing were left on the cutting room floor before the movies were released to the public. However, refusing to concede entirely to the censors, West developed a novel method of expressing her trademark sexy style. While she no longer included words and actions that were explicitly prohibited by the Production Code, her delivery of seemingly innocent material often implied another layer of meaning that was just as scandalous as the content that had previously been censored. Audiences flocked to the theaters to see her movies, taking pleasure in her clever defiance of the powerful censors.

Another way that artists, entertainers, and others defy censorship is by using unauthorized avenues to distribute their material. Free speech analyst Nan Levinson writes about this phenomenon and asserts that "banning the unpalatable merely drives it underground."[1] A prime example of this is the alternative comic-book movement that developed during the 1960s and 70s. Comic books came under fire around the mid-1950s because parents became concerned about the graphic depictions of violence, sex, and drug abuse that their children were looking at. Psychiatrist Fredric Wertham spearheaded an effort for more stringent regulations of comic-book content, and the U.S. Congress launched an investigation into the industry. To calm the public outcry, publishers of comic books decided to censor their own products and developed the Comics Code Authority to enforce limitations on the depiction of violence and illicit activity. It became virtually impossible for comic-book artists to get publishers to distribute any work that did not comply with the code.

This censorship motivated some artists to rebel and create an entirely new genre of comic books. They began to self-publish their work by printing it in their homes or garages and distributing it by word of mouth or by selling it in the hangouts popular with the counterculture of the era, such as head shops that sold drug paraphernalia, psychedelic posters, and underground newspapers. To distinguish their work from mainstream comic books, these maverick publishers called the new genre "underground comix" and often directly addressed the very subjects that were banned by major publishers.

Censorship can also boomerang when it mobilizes those who are censored (and like-minded allies) to expend a tremendous amount of time, energy, and resources to publicly protest the banning of their work. If the resistance gains enough support, the censoring body is forced to deal with considerable community opposition. One case that clearly illustrates this phenomenon is the struggle that took place between the CBS television network and Tommy Smothers of the breakout *Smothers Brothers* television variety show. In 1967 Tommy and his brother Dickie were recruited by CBS to create a show that would lure youthful viewers away from *Bonanza*, the popular NBC western. Perhaps the conservative CBS executives felt that they had created a monster, because the Smothers brothers excelled at appealing to baby boomers by addressing controversial subjects like the Vietnam War and the civil rights movement.

The show's cultural criticism and satirical comedy routines made the network nervous, and they began to edit or cut any sketches that criticized the government and celebrated the growing countercultural youth movement. When the CBS censors refused to air the guest performance of folk singer Pete Seeger singing a ballad that compared an inept World War II officer to President Lyndon B. Johnson, Tommy Smothers made his battle with CBS public. He reported the censorship to any newspaper, magazine, or radio station that would listen to him. Historian Aniko Bodroghkozy writes that Smothers's move "caused a public uproar. Popular-press accounts were generally sympathetic to the Smothers and Seeger and critical of the network's actions."[2] Thousands of viewers sent letters of protest to CBS. The pressure finally caused CBS to retract its position and allow Seeger to sing the song on a later show. After losing this struggle, the network began to allow more politically charged material into its programs. The persistence of Tommy Smothers eventually helped to open the airways to a greater diversity of viewpoints.

Clearly, censoring any form of expression is extremely difficult because there are always people who disagree that a given publication, TV show, or other depiction is harmful and should be banned. Historian Alfred Whitney Griswold argues that "books won't stay banned. They won't burn. Ideas won't go to jail. In the long run of history, the censor and the inquisitor have always lost. The only weapon against bad ideas is better ideas."[3] Most acts of censorship produce ongoing struggles among divergent factions that bring additional attention to censored material and issues concerning freedom of expression. In *History of Issues: Censorship*, the authors explore how the debate over censorship has evolved from colonial days to the twenty-first century. They look closely at the controversy over government censorship during wartime, how the development of technology has affected the issue of free speech, and various debates over freedom of expression in popular culture—including art, movies, and books. The selections show that censorship has been a vital topic of contention throughout American history.

Notes

1. Nan Levinson, "A Democracy of Voices: Free Expression in the U.S.," *Andy Warhol Foundation for the Visual Arts*, August 1997. www.warholfoundation.org/artcult .htm.
2. Aniko Bodroghkozy, *Groove Tube: Sixties Television and the Youth Rebellion*. Durham, NC: Duke University Press, 2001, p. 125.
3. Alfred Whitney Griswold, *New York Times*, February 24, 1959, quoted in the *Quote Garden*, 2006. www.quotegarden.com/censorship.html.

CHAPTER 1

Early American Censorship Struggles

Chapter Preface

Although the printing press arrived in America in 1636, the first regularly published newspaper did not appear until 1704. It did not take the colonists long to understand the value of the press in their small settlements, and by 1730 weekly newspapers thrived in almost every colony. These quickly became the principal source of news and an esteemed forum for public debate. It is therefore not surprising that some of the first struggles over censorship in America concerned the colonial press.

One of the most famous cases of censorship to occur before the American colonies gained independence from Britain was the trial of John Peter Zenger. An immigrant from Germany, Zenger set up his printing business in New York and began publishing the popular *New York Weekly Journal: containing the freshest Advices, Foreign and Domestic* in 1733. Zenger's opposition party newspaper competed with the (British) government-sanctioned *New York Weekly Gazette*. When he published articles attacking Governor William Cosby of New York, the governor brought charges of seditious libel on the printer and had him jailed.

As historians Jonathon Green and Nicholas Karolides explain in their *Encyclopedia of Censorship*, the convention at the time was that it was a severe offence to reveal true scandals because the people involved would likely be incited to seek revenge and thus disturb the peace. The motto of the era was "the greater the truth, the greater the libel." Zenger's trial was unique because his lawyers argued that publishing the truth should be protected as the rightful freedom of the press. After demanding a jury trial, the lawyers profited from the growing anti-British sentiment in the colonies and won the case. The argument set a precedent for later trials over censorship, and the persecution of Zenger became a rallying cry for freedom of the press and independence from Britain in the colonies.

Another significant censorship struggle in early America was fought over moral values. Perhaps no single man had more influence in this battle than Anthony Comstock, who sought to eliminate obscenity and criminalize abortion and birth control at the turn of the twentieth century. As the relentless leader of the New York Society for the Suppression of Vice, Comstock campaigned against sensational newspapers, dime novels written for boys, romance novels written for girls, nudity in art, public lectures discussing sexuality, contraceptive devices, pamphlets about birth control, and a host of other material. Between 1872 and 1874, Comstock and his followers seized over 130,000 pounds of books and 60,300 miscellaneous items to prevent their distribution to the public.

Comstock quickly became a celebrity in Washington D.C. In 1873 he lobbied Congress to pass stringent laws against sending or advertising "obscene" materials through the mail. President Ulysses Grant named him a special postal inspector and gave him the official power to censor material. Up until his death in 1915, Comstock used the position to confiscate books and art, arrest booksellers and public lecturers, raid art schools employing nude models, and jail anyone selling birth control. His organization was responsible for arresting more than 1,200 people in fifteen years. Due to his influence, many states passed their own versions of what were called "Comstock Laws" and started their own societies "for the suppression of vice." Due to the influence of Anthony Comstock, cultural censorship had become well entrenched by the 1920s.

Press Censorship in the Colonies

David A. Copeland

In the following selection scholar David A. Copeland describes early American struggles over freedom of the press. Freedom of speech was a critical issue for most colonists who came to America to escape religious persecution and monarchical rule. Nevertheless, Copeland notes, the colonists were subject to British laws that outlawed criticism of the government and other kinds of speech. By 1735, however, the colonies had enough power to resist British rule and openly condemn tyrannical laws and government limits on the press. Copeland also includes several excerpts from colonial newspapers addressing censorship and freedom of the press. Copeland is a professor of mass communications at Emory and Henry College in Emory, Virginia, and is the author of many books and articles about American colonial journalism, including Debating the Issues in Colonial Newspapers: Primary Documents on Events of the Period.

When an American hears the terms freedom of the press and freedom of speech, his or her thoughts turn immediately to the First Amendment, which reads, "Congress shall make no laws . . . abridging the freedom of speech, or of the press." Not all people, however, interpret the First Amendment in the same way. Some people believe that because the amendment states "no laws," no constraints should be placed on media or the speech of anyone. Most people believe that the media's rights guaranteed by the First Amendment should be balanced with other rights enjoyed by Americans.

Freedom of Speech in the Colonies

The concept of what media may print or broadcast is constantly undergoing revision. The ultimate decision of what receives protection under the First Amendment comes from rulings made by the U.S. Supreme Court. Any notion that we might have of what freedom of the press means for media today would have been unacceptable to almost all Americans living in the colonial period. Americans operated under British law, under which many kinds of speech were illegal, especially criticism of government. Most American colonists believed in freedom of speech and the press. Many of the settlers who colonized what would become the United States came here to escape religious persecution, and they talked and wrote of free speech in relation to their rights to publish religious material that supported their understanding of the Bible.

Dissension from the religious rules set up in America by groups such as the Puritans occurred in the colonies just as it did in England. Because of this criticism, England established laws that required printers to have all that they printed approved by government officials. Known as licensing, all colonial governors received directions in 1686 "that no person keep any printing-press for printing, nor that any book, pamphlet, or other matter whatsoever be printed without your especiall leave and license first obtained."

In 1690 printer Benjamin Harris violated that law. Harris, who came to America the same year that the licensing law went into effect, believed that Boston needed a newspaper so that its citizens could be kept apprised of all events that affected them. On September 25, 1690, he published *Publick Occurrences Both Forreign and Domestick*. The three-page newspaper contained no attacks on the licensing law or complaints about the government; it simply related to its readers what was going on—a smallpox outbreak, a murder, a good harvest among the "Christianized" Indians, the execution of Native American prisoners of war, and a report that the king of

France, Louis XIV, might be sleeping with his son's wife. Massachusetts officials would probably never have approved the printing of the last two items, and therein lay the problem for Harris. His publication and its contents were never approved by the governor. On September 29, the governor ordered that Harris never publish *Publick Occurrences* again. America's first newspaper printed but one issue before it died at the censor's hand.

Newspaper success in the early eighteenth century was tied directly to governmental approval of content, but the idea that a newspaper needed the endorsement of a political body did not last long. Printers of Boston's *New-England Courant* and Philadelphia's *American Weekly Mercury* both experienced run-ins with the authorities in the early 1720s when the printers published material critical of some aspect of leadership in their colony.

One-Sided Freedom of the Press

By 1735 America's colonies had grown large enough to foster political dissension. No longer was press control proposed for religious reasons. The trial of John Peter Zenger revolved around who would control New York politics. Zenger's paper, the *New-York Weekly Journal*, attacked the government of Governor William Cosby and defended its right to do so as freedom of the press. Another New York printer, James Parker, defied the colony's government and published objectionable material in 1747. In 1756 Parker called into question the results of an election. He defended his right to do so as freedom of the press. Slowly, Americans were developing the concept of freedom of the press as a means of checking government actions, stirring agitation for causes, and fighting laws some believed to be tyrannical. When England attempted to impose a tax on paper in 1765, the colonists, regarding the tax as an attack on American freedoms, erupted in protest.

By the 1770s, newspapers were regarded as a principal instrument in the fight for freedom from England, but not all printers thought independence was proper. Tory printers, who felt America should remain part of Britain, found their presses destroyed and their likenesses hanged in effigy by angry Patriots who supported America's separation from Great Britain. Even though the majority of Americans demanded a free press to criticize government, minority opposition was often suppressed. Freedom of the press—even though it had left behind religious restraints—was still meant principally for those in control. The *Massachusetts Spy* proclaimed in 1772, "However lordly fools would be!! FOREVER shall the PRESS be FREE!!" But the author of the lines no doubt never intended that the "fools" be given press access to espouse opposing viewpoints, even though many printers in the 1770s claimed they believed in the concept of an open and unbiased press by declaring in their nameplates that their papers were "Open to all Parties, but Influenced by None," as did printer John Pinkney's *Virginia Gazette.*

Even if printers consciously limited the information presented in their newspapers to one side of an issue, publishing articles that called for limiting free speech were rare. This [selection] includes one newspaper essay from the 1730s that explains why limiting the press was necessary. It also contains two pieces from the 1770s that call for limiting press freedom, one an essay in the pro-British newspaper the *Censor,* the other a letter from a person signing himself "Tory." Both attack the freedom of the press as it was used by American Patriots to attack British officials when these same Patriots used whatever means possible to silence Tory or Loyalist publications.

Examples from Colonial Newspapers

[The excerpts that follow begin] with a selection of pieces advocating limitations on freedom of the press. The first two are statements by seventeenth-century policymakers, Virginia Governor William Berkeley in 1671 and the Massachusetts Bay governing council in 1690. The section ends with a statement by jurist Francis Hopkinson on the dangers of criticizing government, which includes self-interest, partisanship, and sedition.

A selection of pieces defending freedom of the press begins with an essay that appeared over a four-week period in the *Pennsylvania Gazette* in 1737. The author of the essay was probably James Alexander, the person behind the printed attacks on New York Governor William Cosby in 1733 and 1734. Alexander wrote in response to essays from Barbados criticizing the trial of John Peter Zenger. This piece is followed by a series of essays on freedom of speech and of the press printed by Benjamin Edes and John Gill after they assumed control of the *Boston Gazette* in April 1755. The series included "An Apology for the LIBERTY of the PRESS" and was probably printed by the Patriot-minded printers to establish the agenda of the paper under their tenure. The series is followed by a 1767 *Boston Gazette* essay that may well have been a collaboration with the printers' good friend Samuel Adams. Adams, Edes, and Gill were outspoken opponents of British intervention in the colonies. While the three advocated free speech and a free press, their opponents claimed "they would confine it wholly to themselves." The [article] closes with a *New-Hampshire Gazette* statement on the value of a free press to society shortly before the signing of the Declaration of Independence.

In Favor of Censorship and Press Limitations

William Berkeley: "Enquiries to the Governor of Virginia." British law required colonial governors to issue reports on the state of their colonies and to reply to any questions that might arise concerning the colonies. In 1671 the Lords Commissioners of Foreign Plantations sent Virginia Governor William Berkeley a questionnaire on the state of religion in his province. In his reply, the governor lamented the fact that religious life in Virginia could be better, and he added the statement below on the state of the press there. Berkeley's statement accurately describes the perception of most colonial governments on the potential dangers of a press not controlled by government licensing, especially in matters of religion and politics.

"Enquiries to the Governor of Virginia," 1671

I thank God, there are no free schools nor printing; and I hope we shall not have these hundred years; for learning has brought disobedience, and heresy, and sects into the world, and printing has divulged them, and libels against the government. God keep us from both!

William Berkeley

The Governor's Council of Massachusetts: "The Suppression of Publick Occurrences." The political situation in Boston during 1690 was chaotic. Taxpayers had revolted against the colony's policies, the French and their Indian allies were at war with the British, and many of the farms and plantations throughout the colony lay in ruin. In order to separate rumor from fact, Benjamin Harris began a newspaper, *Publick Occurrences*. Four days after its publication, the governing council ordered the newspaper suppressed and Harris never again to print a newspaper in Massachusetts. The decree stated that any future printing must be licensed by the colony's government. As a result, the newspapers printed in Boston that followed *Publick Occurrences* carried "Printed by Authority" in their nameplates.

By the Governour & Council,

Whereas some have lately presumed to Print and Disperse a Pamphlet Entitled. Publick Occurrences, both Forreign and Domestick: Boston, Thursday, Septemb. 25th. 1690. *Without the least Privity or Countenance of Authority.*

The Governour and Council having had the perusal of the said Pamphlet, and finding that therein is contained Reflections of a very high nature: As also sundry doubtful and uncertain Reports, do hereby manifest and declare their high Resentment and Disallowance of said Pamphlet, and Order that the same be Suppressed and called in; strickly forbidding any person or persons for the future to Set forth any thing in Print without License first obtained from those that are or shall be appointed by the Government to grant the same.

By Order of the Governour & Council. Isaac Addington, Secr. Published in Boston, September 29th, 1690.

An Anonymous New Yorker: "The Dangers of Papers and Pamphlets." In January 1734, the assault on New York Governor William Cosby by writers in the *New-York Weekly Journal* was at full force. The attack on Cosby was part of a political power play in the colony, and citizens lined up on both sides of the argument. In this selection, an anonymous writer requests that printer William Bradford run an essay that the writer claims comes from the pen of Joseph Addison, the British satirist and printer of a much-emulated London newspaper, the *Spectator*. Addison's words were most often used to support the concept of freedom of the press, but here, a selection has been gleaned that points out the dangers of allowing printers to publish newspapers and pamphlets without any governmental control.

New-York Gazette, 28 January 1733 (1734)

THERE is nothing so scandalous to a Government, and detestable in the Eyes of all good Men, as defamatory Papers and Pamphlets; but at the same Time there is nothing so difficult to tame, as a Satyrical Author. An angry Writer, who cannot appear in Print, naturally vents his Spleen in Libels and Lampoons. . . .

IT has been proposed, *to oblige every Person that writes a Book, or a Paper, to swear himself the Author of it, and enter down in this a publick Register his Name and Place of abode.*

THIS, indeed, would have effectually suppressed all printed Scandal, which generally appears under borrowed Names, or under none at all. But it is to be feared, that such an Expedient would not only destroy Scandal, but Learning. It would operate promiscuously, and root up the Corn and Tares together. Not to mention some of the most celebrated Works of Piety, which have preceeded from Anonymous Authors, who have made it their Merit to convey to us so great a Charity in secret: There are few Works of Genius that come out at first with the Author's Name. The Writer generally makes a Tryal of them in the World before he owns them; and, I believe, very few, who are capable of Writing, would let Pen to Paper, if they knew, before hand, that they must not publish their Productions but on such Conditions. For my own part, I must declare the Papers I present . . . shall last no longer than while the Author is concealed. . . .

I have never yet heard of a Ministry, who have inflicted an exemplary Punishment on an Author that has supported their Cause with Falshood and Scandal, and treated in a most cruel manner, the Names of those who have been looked upon as their Rivals and Antagonists. Would a Government set an everlasting Mark of their Displeasure upon one of those infamous Writers, who makes his Court to them by tearing to Pieces the Reputation of a Competitor, we should quickly see an End put to this Rate of Vermin, that are a Scandal to Government, and a Reproach to Human Nature. . . .

I cannot but look upon the finest Strokes of Satyr which are aimed at *particular Persons*, and which are supported even with the Appearance of Truth, to be the Marks of an evil Mind, and highly Criminal in themselves. Infamy, like other punishments, is under the Direction and Distribution of the *Magistrate*, and not of any private *Person*. Accordingly we learn from a Fragment of Cicero, that tho' there were very few Capital Punishments in the Twelve Tables, a

Libel or Lampoon which took away the *good Names* of another, was to be punished by Death.

BUT this is far from being our Case. Our Satyr is nothing but *Ribaldry*, and *Bilingsgate*. Scurrilty passes for Wit; and he who can call Names in the greatest Variety of Phrase, is looked upon to have the shrewdest Pen. By this Means the Honour of Families is ruined, the *highest Posts* and greatest Titles are render'd cheap and vile in the Sight of the People; the noblest Virtues, and most exalted Parts, exposed to the Contempt of the Vicious and Ignorant. Should a Foreigner, who knows nothing of our private Factions, or one who is to act his part in the World, when our present *Heats and Animosities are forgot*, should, I say, such an one form to himself a Notion of the greatest Men of all Sides in the *British* Nation, who are now suffering from the Characters which are given them in some or most of those abominable Writings which are daily published among us, what a Nation of Monsters must we appear!

AS this cruel Practice tends to the utter Subversion of all Truth and Humanity among us, it deserves the utmost Detestation and Discouragement of all who have either the Love of their Country, or the Honour of their Religion, at Heart. I would therefore earnestly recommend it to the Consideration of those who deal in these pernicious Arts of Writing. . . . Every honest Man sets as high a Value upon a *good Name*, as upon Life it self; and I cannot but think that those who privily assault the one, would destroy the other, might they do it with the same *Secrecy and Impunity*.

An Anonymous Bostonian: "Condemnation of the Party Press." Following the Boston Massacre in 1770, divisions along political lines in Boston became obvious in the press. The sole purpose of one newspaper, the *Censor*, was to support the policies of the British administration of the colony. As a result, the newspaper's writers, who wrote in anonymity, attacked the partisan nature of the writings that appeared in some Boston newspapers, particularly the *Boston Gazette*. The essay suggests that the rise of partisanship is synonymous with lies and threats to legitimate government. As a result, freedom of the press must be controlled. It is worth noting that although this essay was unsigned, its author may well have been Massachusetts Lieutenant Governor Peter Oliver or Dr. Benjamin Church. Church, who was appointed surgeon general of America at the start of the Revolution, was later confined because of correspondence with the British army that occupied Boston.

The Censor (Boston), 7 March 1772

THE advantages resulting from the art of Printing are acknowledged to be as important and interesting to mankind, as from any mechanical invention, as no method is so well fitted to preserve the production of the learned, and to extend useful knowledge to every order of the species with such surprizing facility and exactness; an art unknown to the ancients. . . . So long as the Press is directed to the valuable purposes of extending literature, promoting arts, improving the morals and correcting the vices of mankind, so long it hath a just claim to the patronage of every friend to science and liberty: But if, by the ascendency and influence of a *party*, it becomes a vehicle in the hands of the licentious to calumniate the amiable and virtuous, and by insidious arts to create fears, jealousies, and distractions, to the great interruption of publick peace and happiness; such prostitution of the Press I am persuaded every judicious man must condemn; and wish that measures might be taken to prevent. I am constrained to say, that no country hath so wantonly abused the freedom of the Press as this; on this account it is notorious.

Francis Hopkinson: "When Government Can Suppress the Press." Philadelphia lawyer Francis Hopkinson signed the Declaration of Independence and was a member of the Constitutional Convention, but in 1776 he used "Tory" as a pen name to write a letter supporting press suppression. Hopkinson believed, as did many Patriots, that freedom of the press was needed in America, but he also believed that there were limits on what could be said. In this letter, he defines those limits to any threat that might undermine the foundations of government.

Pennsylvania Evening Post (Philadelphia), 16 November 1776

The liberty of the press hath been justly held up as an important privilege of the people. . . . But when this privilege is manifestly abused, and the press becomes an engine for sowing the most dangerous dissensions, for spreading false alarms, and undermining the very foundations of government, ought be not that government, upon the plain principles of self-preservation, to silence by its own authority, such a daring violator of its peace, and tear from its bosom the serpent that would sting it to death.

A Tory

Defending Freedom of the Press

Andrew Hamilton: "A Principal Pillar of a Free Government." Andrew Hamilton defended John Peter Zenger in his famous libel trial in 1735. . . , but other than Zenger's own printings, nothing about the trial appeared in American newspapers until years later. That does not mean that printers did not discuss the free press ramifications of the trial. In this extended essay, which appeared over four weeks in the *Pennsylvania Gazette*, an unsigned essay describes the value of freedom of press and speech for the success of government by placing the concepts into a historical concept. In it, the author emphasizes the concept of truth in printing, the mainstay in the Zenger defense. Even though printer Benjamin Franklin did not attribute the essay to Hamilton, who in addition to being a lawyer was an elected Philadelphia official, the *Barbados Gazette* named Hamilton its author when it reprinted the essay in January 1738.

Pennsylvania Gazette (Philadelphia), 17 November 1737–8 December 1737To the author of the Pennsylvania Gazette

SIR,

THE FREEDOM OF SPEECH is a *principal Pillar* in a free Government: when this support is taken away the Constitution is dissolved, and Tyranny is erected on its Ruins. Republics and limited Monarchies derive their Strength and Vigor from a *popular Examination* into the Actions of the Magistrates. This Privilege in all Ages has been and always will be abused. The best Princes could not escape the Censure and Envy of the Times they lived in. But the Evil is not so great as it may appear at first Sight. A Magistrate who sincerely aims at the *Good* of the Society will always have the Inclinations of a great Majority on his side; and impartial Posterity will not fail to render him Justice.

These Abuses of the Freedom of Speech are the Excrescences of Liberty. They ought to be suppressed; but to whom dare we commit the Care of doing it? An evil Magistrate entrusted with the POWER to *punish Words* is armed with a WEAPON the most *destructive* and *terrible*. Under pretense of pruning off the exuberant Branches, he frequently destroys the Tree. . . .

Augustus Caesar under the specious Pretext of preserving the Characters of the Romans from Defamation introduced the Law whereby Libeling was involved in the Penalties of *Treason* against the State. . . .

Henry VII, a Prince mighty in Politics, procured that ACT to be passed whereby the Jurisdiction of the Star Chamber was confirmed and extended. . . . The Subjects were terrified from uttering their Griefs while they saw the Thunder of the Star Chamber pointed at their Heads. This Caution, however, could not prevent several dangerous Tumults and Insurrections. For when the Tongues of the People are restrained, they commonly discharge their Resentments by a more *dangerous Organ*, and break out into open Acts of Violence.

During the Reign of Henry VIII ... every light Expression which happened to displease him was construed by his supple Judges into a Libel, sometimes extended to high Treason....

IN the two former Papers the Writer endeavored to prove by historical Facts the fatal Dangers that necessarily attend a Restraint on Freedom of Speech and the Liberty of the Press: Upon which the following Reflection naturally occurs, viz., *that whoever attempts to suppress either of those,* OUR NATURAL RIGHTS, *ought to be regarded as an* ENEMY *to liberty and the constitution. An Inconveniency is always to be suffered when it cannot be removed without introducing a Worse....*

To infuse the Minds of the People an ill Opinion of a just Administration is a Crime that deserves no Mercy: But to expose the evil Designs or weak Management of a Magistrate is the Duty of every Member of Society.... No Law could be better framed to prevent People from publishing their Thoughts on the Administration than that which makes no distinction whether a Libel be true or false....

The Punishment for writing Truth is Pillory, loss of Ears, branding the Face with hot Irons, Fine and Imprisonment at the Discretion of the Court. Nay, the Punishment is to be heightened in proportion to the Truth of the Facts contained in the Libel....

Upon the Whole. To suppress Enquiries into the Administration is good Policy in an arbitrary Government: But a free Constitution and freedom of Speech have such a reciprocal Dependence on each other that they cannot subsist without consisting together.

W.K.: *"Of Freedom of Speech."* When Benjamin Edes and John Gill bought the *Boston Gazette* in 1755, the pair opened publication with a series of letters and essays on the significance of the freedom of speech and the press. The letter written by the unnamed W.K. was probably taken from an English newspaper, or it may have been produced by the printers. Either way, its appearance was to let readers know the stance of the paper's new owners. In this letter, freedom of press and speech are equated with the preservation of liberty.

Boston Gazette, or Country Journal, 21 April 1755

Of Freedom of SPEECH.

WITHOUT Freedom of Thought, there can be no such Thing as Wisdom, and no such Thing as publick Liberty, without Freedom of Speech: Which is the Right of every Man, as far as by it he does not hurt and controul the Right of another; and this is the only Check which it ought to suffer, the only Bounds which it ought to know.

This sacred Privilege is so essential to free Government, that the Security of Property: and the Freedom of Speech, always go together; and in those wretched Countries where a Man cannot call his Tongue his own. Whoever would overthrow the Liberty of the Nation, must begin by subduing the Freedom of Speech; a Thing terrible to publick Traytors. . . .

Freedom of Speech, therefore, being of such infinite Importance to the Preservation of Liberty, every one who loves Liberty ought to encourage Freedom of Speech.

An Anonymous London Writer: "An Apology for the Liberty of the Press." Boston printers Edes and Gill continued their series supporting free speech and press freedom through their first nine issues in 1755. In this essay, taken from a London newspaper, the concept that all Englishmen are born with these rights is declared.

Boston Gazette, or Country Journal, 26 May 1755

An Apology for the Liberty of the Press

THE Freedom of the Press, by which I mean the *Freedom which every Subject has to communicate his Sentiments to the Publick, in that Manner, which may make them most universally known,* is a Freedom which does not proceed from any

Peculiarity in the Frame of the *English* Constitution, but is essential to and coeval with all free Governments, into which it is not adopted, but born.

. . . the people of *England* without *the Liberty of the Press* to inform them of the fitness and unfitness of measures, approv'd or condem'd by those whom they have trusted, and whom they may trust again, would be in as blind a state of subjection, as if they lived under the most arbitrary and inquisitorial government; nay their condition would be aggravated by the melancholly consideration, that they lent their own helping hands both to forge and rivet their chains.

Freeborn American: "The Nature of Political Liberty." In 1767 Americans were abuzz with talk of a new set of taxes about to be imposed upon them. Named collectively for Charles Townshend, Chancellor of the Exchequer (treasury), the new duties taxed tea, paint, lead, paper, and glass. The *Boston Gazette* served as the principal voice of protest against British taxes in New England. Here, the anonymous writer asserts that freedom of speech is essential to the preservation of liberty.

Boston Gazette, and Country Journal, 9 March 1767

Man, in a state of nature, has undoubtedly a right to speak and act without controul. In a state of civil society, that right is limited by the law—Political liberty consists in a freedom of speech and action, so far as the laws of a community will permit, and no farther: all beyond is criminal, and tends to the destruction of Liberty itself.—That society whose laws least restrain the words and actions of its members, is most free.—There is no nation on the earth, where freedom of speech is more extensive than among the English: This is what keeps the constitution in health and vigour, and is in a great measure the cause of our preservation as a free people: For should it ever be dangerous to exercise this privilege, it is easy to see, without the spirit of prophecy, slavery, and bondage would soon be the portion of Britons.

Freeborn American

Robert Fowle: "A Sacred Right." Late in 1775, printer Robert Fowle established a newspaper in Exeter to serve as a voice for Tories in New Hampshire. Like many other printers with British leanings during the Revolutionary period, Fowle found it necessary to print statements on freedom of the press as a way to justify the rights of all printers and citizens—despite their political positions—to publish newspapers or have letters and essays printed. In this statement, Fowle sees free speech as a sacred right. Without it, he believes, all freedoms and privileges that Americans love will be lost.

New-Hampshire Gazette (Exeter), 25 May 1776

The liberty of the Press has ever been held as one of the most sacred rights of a free people, and when we are abridged of that invaluable priviledge, farewell to Peace, Liberty, and safety, farewell to Learning Knowledge and Truth, farewell all that is dear to us; we must ever after grope in darkness, thick darkness, that may even be felt: may Heaven forbid such deprivation, and long continue to us this invaluable blessing.

Anthony Comstock Crusades to Eradicate Obscenity

Mary Alden Hopkins

In the following selection, first published on May 22, 1915, in Harper's Weekly *magazine, Mary Alden Hopkins interviews Anthony Comstock. In 1823 Comstock had created the New York Society for the Suppression of Vice, an organization dedicated to censoring bawdy literature and other materials that Comstock and his followers deemed immoral. As his influence grew, he convinced Congress to pass the Comstock laws, which outlawed the delivery of "obscene, lewd, or lascivious" material through the U.S. mail. For Comstock, obscene material included any information pertaining to birth control and even some anatomy textbooks. Over the course of his career, he was responsible for destroying over 160 tons of books and pictures. While he had many supporters until his death (shortly after this interview in 1915), he also had many adversaries who believed his tactics compromised the civil liberties of American citizens. After Comstock attempted to censor his play* Mrs. Warren's Profession, *British playwright George Bernard Shaw coined the term* Comstockery *to ridicule what he saw as Comstock's overblown hysteria over perceived obscenity.*

In this selection, Comstock explains how he became a devoted anti-vice crusader for the welfare of youth. He also describes his belief that obscene images and literature interfere with the proper character development of young people, encouraging them to engage in criminal behavior. To protect young minds from dangerous influences, Comstock writes it is necessary to outlaw the distribution of obscene material.

Hopkins was an early-twentieth-century journalist and author of several books, including Hanna Moore and Her Circle.

Mary Alden Hopkins, "Birth Control and Public Morals: An Interview with Anthony Comstock," *Harper's Weekly*, May 22, 1915.

"Have read your articles. Self control and obedience to Nature's laws, you seem to overlook. Let men and women live a life above the level of the beasts. I see nothing in either of your articles along these lines. Existing laws are an imperative necessity in order to prevent the downfall of youths of both sex," wrote Mr. Anthony Comstock, secretary of the New York Society for the Suppression of Vice, replying to my request for an interview on the subject of Birth Control.

During the interview which he kindly allowed me, he reiterated his belief in the absolute necessity of drastic laws.

"To repeal the present laws would be a crime against society," he said, "and especially a crime against young women."

Anthony Comstock's Cause

Although the name Anthony Comstock is known all over the country and over most of the civilized world, few people know for exactly what Mr. Comstock stands and what he has accomplished. It has been the policy of those who oppose his work to speak flippantly of it and to minimize his results. The Society for the Suppression of Vice was formed to support Mr. Comstock, from the beginning he has been its driving force, and it is giving him only the credit that is due him to say that the tremendous accomplishments of the society in its fight against various publications in the past forty years have been in reality the accomplishments of Mr. Comstock.

Up to 1914, Mr. Comstock had caused to be arraigned in state and federal courts 3,697 persons, of whom 2,740 were either convicted or pleaded guilty. On these were imposed fines to the extent of $237,134.30 and imprisonments to the length of 565 years, 11 months, and 20 days.

To this remarkable record of activity can be added since that date 176 arrests and 141 convictions.

The story of how Mr. Comstock began his unusual profession is as interesting as the story of any of the famous captains of industry. He has, if one may borrow a stage term, "created" his unique position.

Obscene Literature

"My attention was first drawn to the publication of vile books forty-three years ago when I was a clerk here in New York City," said Mr. Comstock.

"There was in existence at that time a kind of circulating library where my fellow clerks went, made a deposit, and received the vilest literature, and after reading it, received back the deposit or took other books. I saw young men being debauched by this pernicious influence.

"On March 2nd, 1872, I brought about the arrest of seven persons dealing in obscene books, pictures, and articles. I found that there were 169 books some of which had been in circulation since before I was born and which were publicly advertised and sold in connection with articles for producing abortion, prevention of conception, articles to aid seductions, and for indiscreet and immoral use. I had four publishers dealing in these arrested and the plates for 167 of these books destroyed. The other two books dropped out of sight. I have not seen a copy of one of them for forty years."

From this time on Mr. Comstock devoted his attention to this work, although it was, as he once said, like standing at the mouth of a sewer. Several times men whom he has arrested have later tried to kill him.

There were no laws covering this ostracized business at that time. In March, 1873, Mr. Comstock secured the passage of stringent federal laws closing the mails and the ports to this atrocious business. Two days afterwards, upon the request of certain Senators, Mr. Comstock was appointed Special Agent of the Post Office Department to enforce these laws. He now holds the position of Post Office Inspector. The federal law as it at present stands is as follows:

United States Criminal Code, Section 211.

(Act of March 4th, 1909, Chapter 321, Section 211, United States Statutes at Large, vol. 35, part 1, page 1088 et seq.)

Every obscene, lewd, or lascivious and every filthy book, pamphlet, picture, paper, letter, writing, print, or other publication of an indecent character, and every article or thing designated, adapted or intended for preventing conception or procuring abortion, or for any indecent or immoral use; and every article, instrument, substance, drugs, medicine, or thing which is advertised or described in a manner calculated to lead another to use or apply it for preventing conception or producing abortion, or for any indecent or immoral purpose; and every written or printed card, circular, book, pamphlet, advertisement or notice or any kind giving information, directly, or indirectly, where or how, or by what means any of the hereinbefore mentioned matters, articles or things may be obtained or made, or where or by whom any act or operation of any kind for the procuring or producing of abortion will be done or performed, or how or by what means conception may be prevented or abortion produced, whether sealed or unsealed, and even letter, packet or package or other mail matter containing any filthy, vile or indecent thing, device or substance; and every paper, writing, advertisement or representation that any article, instrument, substance, drug, medicine or thing may, or can be used or applied for preventing conception or producing abortion, or for any indecent or immoral purpose; and every description calculated to induce or incite a person to so use or apply any such article, instrument, substance, drug, medicine or thing, is hereby declared to be non-mailable matter and shall not be conveyed in the mails or delivered from any post office or by any letter carrier. Whosoever shall knowingly deposit or cause to be deposited for mailing or delivery, anything declared by this section to be non-mailable, or shall knowingly take, or cause the same to be taken, from the mails for the purpose of circulating or disposing thereof, or of aiding in the circulation or disposition of the same, shall be fined not more than $5000, or imprisoned not more than five years, or both.

Any one who has the patience to read through this carefully drawn law will see that it covers—well, everything. The detailed accuracy with which it is constructed partly explains Mr. Comstock's almost uniform success in securing convictions. One possible loophole suggested itself to me.

Protecting Youth and Children

"Does it not," I asked, "allow the judge considerable leeway in deciding whether or not a book or a picture is immoral?"

"No," replied Mr. Comstock, "the highest courts in Great Britain and the United States, have laid down the test in all such matters. What he has to decide is *whether or not it might arouse in young and inexperienced minds, lewd or libidinous thoughts.*"

In these words lies the motive of Mr. Comstock's work—the protection of children under twenty-one. If at times his ban seems to some to be too sweepingly applied it is because his faith looks forward to a time when there shall be in all the world not one object to awaken sensuous thoughts in the minds of young people. He expressed this sense of the terrible danger in which young people stand and his society's duty toward them in his fortieth annual report:

> ... We first of all return thanks to Almighty God, the giver of every good and perfect gift, for the opportunities of service for Him in defense of the morals of the more than forty-two million youths and children twenty-one years of age, or under, in the United States of America. His blessings upon our efforts during the past year call for profound thanksgiving: to Almighty God and for grateful and loyal service in the future.
>
> This Society in a peculiar manner is permitted to stand at a vital and strategic point where the foes to moral purity seek to concentrate their most deadly forces against the in-

lawful abortion, or advertises or holds out representations that it can be so used or applied, or any such description as will be calculated to lead another to so use or apply any such article, recipe, drug, medicine or instrument, or who writes or prints, or causes to be written or printed, a card, circular, pamphlet, advertisement, or notice of any kind, or gives information orally, stating when, where, how or whom, or by what means such an instrument, article, recipe, drug or medicine can be purchased or obtained, or who manufactures any such instrument, article, recipe, drug or medicine, is guilty of a misdemeanor, and shall be liable to the same penalties as provided in section eleven hundred and forty-one of this chapter.

This punishment is a sentence of not less than ten days nor more than one year's imprisonment or a fine not less than fifty dollars or both fine and imprisonment for each offense.

Effects on the Medical Profession

"Do not these laws handicap physicians?" I asked, remembering that this criticism is sometimes made.

"They do not," replied Mr. Comstock emphatically. "No reputable physician has ever been prosecuted under these laws. Have you ever known of one?" I had not, and he continued, "Only infamous doctors who advertise or send their foul matter by mail. A reputable doctor may tell his patient in his office what is necessary, and a druggist may sell on a doctor's written prescription drugs which he would not be allowed to sell otherwise."

This criticism of the laws interfering with doctors is so continually made that I asked again.

"Do the laws ever thwart the doctor's work; in cases, for instance, where pregnancy would endanger a woman's life?"

Mr. Comstock replied with the strongest emphasis:

"A doctor is allowed to bring on an abortion in cases where a woman's life is in danger. And is there anything in these laws that forbids a doctor's telling a woman that pregnancy must not occur for a certain length of time or at all? Can they not use self-control? Or must they sink to the level of the beasts?"

"But," I protested, repeating an argument often brought forward, although I felt as if my persistence was somewhat placing me in the ranks of those who desire evil rather than good, "If the parents lack that self-control, the punishment falls upon the child."

"It does not," replied Mr. Comstock. "The punishment falls upon the parents. When a man and woman marry they are responsible for their children. You can't reform a family in any of these superficial ways. You have to go deep down into their minds and souls. The prevention of conception would work the greatest demoralization. God has set certain natural barriers. If you turn loose the passions and break down that fear you bring worse disaster than the war. It would debase sacred things, break down the health of women and disseminate a greater curse than the plagues and diseases of Europe."

A Lawyer Argues Against Comstock Censorship

Theodore Schroeder

Theodore Schroeder was one of the first attorneys in U.S. history to develop detailed legal arguments in support of First Amendment rights. Schroeder defended civil liberties during the World War I era, when government censorship and repression of dissenters had steadily eroded the right to free expression in America. In spite of the oppressive atmosphere, advocates for women's rights, labor unions, and immigrants bravely tried to put forward their ideas and opinions. Schroeder wrote constitutional defenses for many who were tried in court, including birth control advocate Margaret Sanger, anarchist Emma Goldman, and New York radical Moses Harman. He also fought against the Comstock laws developed by anti-vice crusader Anthony Comstock that outlawed so-called obscene material.

In the following selection first published in 1911, Schroeder asserts that such laws are unconstitutional because they allow an elite few to dictate religious and moral standards to a diverse citizenship. Schroeder was concerned that the strict definitions of obscenity suppressed all information about sexual matters, including reports by doctors about venereal diseases and birth control for women who might die if they had to deliver a baby. Schroeder wrote extensively about constitutional law and was the author of the Free Press Anthology *and* "Obscene" Literature and Constitutional Law. *He helped found the Free Speech League in 1911, an organization that was the precursor to the American Civil Liberties Union.*

My numerous smug friends, who pride themselves on their "eminent respectability," often reproach me gently for my extensive advocacy of freedom of speech and press,

Theodore Schroeder, "Prolegomena," *Obscene Literature and Constitutional Law*, 1911, pp. 7–9.

and of uncensored mails and express. To defend the right of all humans to an opportunity to know all there is to know, even about the subject of sex, to the polluted minds of my "pure" friends, is to defend an "uncleanness"—not at all unclean so far as it relates to their own bodies, but "unclean" to talk and read about—not "unclean" as to any acts or facts in their own lives, but "unclean" only to admit a consciousness of those facts. I reluctantly confess that all such hypocritical moral cant, or diseased sex-sensitiveness, arouses in me the most profound contempt of which my phlegmatic nature is capable. Perhaps that is *one* reason why I was impelled to do this uncompensated and unpopular work and sometimes to do it in a manner that is devoid of tact, according to the judgment of those who dare not countenance robust frankness.

They say to me, "What do you care? You know all you wish to upon the tabooed subject, what do you care, even though the general public is kept in ignorance, and a few [thousand] go insane as the result? That doesn't harm you any, and may be the public is benefited, in that, together with serious and searching sex-discussion, much real smut is also suppressed." Such has always been the specious plea of the shortsighted and the cowardly, during the whole period of the agitation for a secular state and freedom of speech.

Protesting Improper Authority

The answers to such specious "arguments" have been often made in the contests of past centuries, and I can do no better than to quote the answer of Dr. Priestly: "A tax of a penny is a trifle, but a power imposing that tax is never considered as a trifle, because *it may imply absolute servitude in all who submit to it.* In like manner the enjoining of the posture of kneeling at the Lord's supper is not a thing worth disputing about in itself, but *the authority of enjoining it is*; because it is in fact a power of making the Christian religion as burdensome as the Jewish, and a power that hath actually been carried to that length in the church of Rome. Our ancestors, the old Puritans, had the same merit in opposing the imposition of the surplice that Hampden had in opposing the levying of ship money. In neither case was it the thing itself they objected to, so much *as the authority* that enjoined it *and the danger of the precedent.* And it appears to us that the man who is as tenacious of his religious as he is of his civil liberty will oppose them both with equal firmness. The man of a strong and enlarged mind will always oppose these things when only in the beginning, when only the resistance can have any effect; but the weak and the timid, and short-sighted, will attempt nothing till the chains are riveted and resistance is too late. In civil matters the former will take his stand at the levying of the first penny by improper authority, and in matters of religion, at the first, though the most trifling, ceremony that is without reason made necessary, whereas the latter will wait till the load, in both cases, is become too heavy to be either supported or thrown off."

Freedom of the Press

In itself it may not be of great importance that by unconstitutional statutes, much disagreeable literary and inartistic matter about sex is suppressed, nor even that the best scientific literature about sex is withheld from the laity, and to some extent even from physicians: it may not even be of importance that, as a result of this general compulsory ignorance about sex, thousands of people are in asylums who would not be there but for our legalized prudery, and compulsory ignorance, but it is of infinite importance to destroy a precedent which implies the admission of a power to wipe out any literature upon any subject, which, through popular hysteria or party passion, may be declared "against the public welfare."

So long as the present laws against "obscene" literature stand unchallenged as to their constitutionality, we admit that here, as in Russia, liberty of the press is liberty only by permission, not liberty as a matter of right. With the "obscenity" laws as a precedent, our censorship has grown until now . . . liberty of the press in the United States is more perniciously and more extensively curtailed than it was in England at the time of our revolution. That sounds strange to the American dullards who on the Fourth of July *talk* about liberty without knowing its meaning, but a comparison of the laws then and now will justify my conclusion.

THE
HISTORY
OF
ISSUES

CHAPTER 2

Cold War–Era Censorship

comic books with juvenile delinquency. Psychiatrist Fredric Wertham published *Seduction of the Innocent* in 1954, arguing that comic books were harmful to children. He influenced the U.S. Senate to conduct hearings exploring government regulation of comic books. However, the industry decided to censor itself to avoid public opposition. Comic book publishers established the Comics Code Authority (CCA) to restrict violence and sexual explicitness in their publications. The CCA did not completely succeed in censoring all material it considered unacceptable, and "underground" artists began publishing comics that defied the CCA standards. The power of the CCA lessened greatly by the 1980s and 1990s when a host of alternative publishers came on the scene and flourished despite refusing to follow the Code. As of 2005, Archie Comics and two divisions of DC Comics were the only publishers who continued to submit their comic books for CCA approval.

Cold War–Era Censorship

Chapter Preface

The Cold War era began after World War II and was characterized by increasing tension between Western nations led by the United States, and the Communist Bloc led by the Soviet Union. Anti-communist sentiment in America was strong, and political and government organizations and agencies such as the House Un-American Activities Committee (HUAC) and the Federal Bureau of Investigation (FBI), encouraged widespread blacklisting of anyone found to have communist sympathies. Those in opposition saw the blacklisting as official censorship of political dissent.

One of the principle leaders of anti-communism in the 1950s was Senator Joseph Raymond McCarthy of Wisconsin. He used the power of the Senate Permanent Subcommittee on Investigations to investigate American citizens whom he thought were "subversives." Together with the HUAC, the Senate Subcommittee called up members of federal departments, officers and soldiers in the army, and prominent civilians to be scrutinized as political criminals. McCarthy understood how to use the media to his advantage to intensify fears that anyone associated with communism wanted to ruin American life and take over the nation. His tactics were so sensational that "McCarthyism" became a word used to describe charges made without proof and accompanied by exaggerated publicity.

Some of McCarthy's favorite targets were people in the arts and entertainment world. He conducted ongoing hearings that forced hundreds of people to testify before a panel of U.S. politicians. A typical tactic was to threaten them with blacklisting if they refused to appear before the Subcommittee. Most leaders in the arts and entertainment industries—including network television producers and Hollywood directors—abided by the blacklist and refused to hire uncooperative suspects. More than 320 people were placed on the list that stopped them from working in their chosen careers as actors, writers, directors, musicians, artists, and performers. It was a devastating form of censorship for many.

Eventually, many Americans came to see the "McCarthy Hearings" and the blacklisting as a reprehensible form of censorship that victimized hundreds of citizens who were merely trying to exercise their right to freedom of thought and speech. Opponents of the Subcommittee and HUAC began investigating Senator McCarthy and some senators formally condemned McCarthy, who steadily lost influence in government.

During the Cold War era many censorship battles also took place in the cultural arena. One powerful contender in these struggles was the Catholic Church. Since the mid-1930s, the church's citizen organization, the Legion of Decency, had been promoting a strict anti-vice policy, especially in relation to Hollywood motion pictures. When the Motion Picture Producers and Distributors of America (MPPDA) had little success enforcing its Motion Picture Production Code, the Legion enlisted more than 10 million Catholic Americans to sign a pledge to boycott films the Legion deemed to be objectionable. Understanding the influence of the Catholic Church, Hollywood made the Production Code Administration an independent organization and pressured movie production companies to follow the code. The filmmaking requirements included portraying only "correct" standards of life, such as always displaying respect for the law and depicting criminals as unsympathetic. The Production Code Administration held sway over Hollywood until the Supreme Court ruled that movie censorship was a violation of the First Amendment in the landmark case *Burstyn v. Wilson* (1952).

Comic books also came under the scrutiny of censors beginning in the 1950s. As comic books became more popular with young readers, they increasingly included images of violence and crime, leading many adults to link the reading of comic books with juvenile delinquency. Psychiatrist Fredric Wertham published *Seduction of the Innocent* in 1954, arguing that comic books were harmful to children. He influenced the U.S. Senate to conduct hearings exploring government regulation of comic books. However, the industry decided to censor itself to avoid public opposition. Comic book publishers established the Comics Code Authority (CCA) to restrict violence and sexual explicitness in their publications. The CCA did not completely succeed in censoring all material it considered unacceptable, and "underground" artists began publishing comics that defied the CCA standards. The power of the CCA lessened greatly by the 1980s and 1990s when a host of alternative publishers came on the scene and flourished despite refusing to follow the Code. As of 2005, Archie Comics and two divisions of DC Comics were the only publishers who continued to submit their comic books for CCA approval.

Government Repression of Dissent During the Cold War

Jerel A. Rosati

Jerel A. Rosati is a professor of political science and international studies at the University of South Carolina and has written extensively on American foreign and domestic policy. This selection is an excerpt from his analysis of the tensions between civil liberties and national security in twentieth-century America. Rosati documents the culture of conformity and the repressive political atmosphere during the Cold War years in the United States (from the late 1940s to the early 1990s). Although the nation was not officially at war, warlike conditions made many Americans reluctant to criticize government policies that were focused on rooting out the threat of communism.

In the early Cold War years, Senator Joseph R. McCarthy and others exploited the fear of communism to censor and punish those who disagreed with the government or defended constitutional liberties. Rosati writes that government employees were required to take loyalty oaths and that travel to communist countries was restricted in the name of national security. Congressional committees and the FBI conducted investigations to weed out subversives and communists in the military, scientific communities, arts and entertainment industries, and schools and universities. Nevertheless, Rosati points out, censorship and repression during the Cold War period could not quell the growing civil rights and anti–Vietnam War movements of the 1960s and 1970s.

[At] the end of World War II, the civil liberties of Americans were attacked with the onset of the cold war. The strong anticommunist legacy in American history and the

Jerel A. Rosati, *American National Security and Civil Liberties in an Era of Terrorism.* Hampshire, U.K.: Palgrave MacMillan, 2004.

growth of McCarthyism as a political force made communism an enemy to be feared and fought both abroad and at home. McCarthyism represented a broad political coalition of conservative and nativist groups throughout American society. Nothing was immune to their attack, for communists and un-Americanism seemed to be everywhere—within the Truman administration, the government, the Democratic party, in academia and local schools, in Hollywood and the media, and all other walks of life. The anticommunist hysteria, or Red Scare II, became so intense, and the demands of national security overwhelmed the demands of democracy so thoroughly, that even defending the constitutional rights and liberties of Americans was considered evidence of disloyalty—of aiding and abetting the enemy. The domestic politics of anticommunism curtailed the exercise of civil liberties and contributed to the liberal-conservative consensus that provided the foundation for the president's ability to exercise prerogative government in the making of U.S. foreign policy.

It is true that there were some individuals who engaged in espionage for the Soviet Union. It is also true that there were individuals who were members of the Communist Party, USA. [Author Sam Tanenhouse notes that] "Of course, not all Communists attacked their adversaries and only a handful received direct orders from Moscow. The rank and file included many who were engaged in work similar to that of other political activists—attending meetings, distributing leaflets, demonstrating, organizing workers" to promote equality, opportunity, and peace, especially within the United States. Furthermore, communists and sympathizers of the Soviet Union were small in numbers. An overwhelming number of Americans formed the basis of the anticommunist consensus throughout the United States, composition of which contained elites and masses, Democrats and Republicans, liberals and conservatives.

Nevertheless, under the warlike conditions of the cold war many Americans became paranoid and preoccupied with the threat of communism. Criticizing the status quo exposed one to charges of being "unpatriotic," "un-American," and "disloyal." Given this environment, it is easy to see why most liberals moderated their beliefs and behavior to become part of the liberal-conservative consensus. Most Americans learned to go along and "shut up" in public even if they did not fully agree with the dominant beliefs and institutions. This resignation also helps to explain why the cold war years were a period of mass apathy and declining political participation. Clearly, it was a time of great conformity and intolerance in American politics, and these sentiments were driven largely by McCarthyism and the politics of anticommunism. Those who did not conform to the anticommunist norm were often silenced by political repression or lost their legitimacy and credibility.

Government employees were compelled to take "loyalty oaths"; a "secrecy system" was erected to protect classified information; and personnel involved in national security affairs were given lie-detector tests and had their backgrounds investigated. It has been estimated that during the McCarthy era, of a total work force of 65 million, 13 million people were affected by loyalty and security programs. In the name of national security, the government even restricted the number of Americans traveling to communist countries.

In the Name of Security

All these actions were originally intended to protect U.S. national security and respond to congressional investigations of communism in government. However, the "national security ethos" that arose was quickly abused in order to keep information from the public domain and to maximize support throughout society for the government's policies.

Yet the real abuse during the cold war years involved attempts by the government and allied groups throughout society to weed out communists and stifle public dissent in the name of national security. Congressional committees engaged in one investigation after another in an effort to identify and destroy communist influence, and this directly affected people's lives and careers. The attorney general kept a list of hundreds of subversive organizations, making individuals vulnerable to charges of disloyalty if they were affiliated with any of these groups, even if their membership was before or during World War II—and not during the cold war.

David Caute, in *The Great Fear; The Anti-Communist Purge Under Truman and Eisenhower*, documents how thousands of government employees, teachers, labor leaders, journalists, librarians, scientists, writers, and entertainers at national, state, and local levels—virtually all innocent of charges of disloyalty—lost jobs, careers, and reputations as a result of wild accusations and guilt by association. The most celebrated cases, for example, involved people in the movie business that were dismissed and "black listed" from working in major Hollywood studios. Yet, "every segment of society was involved. From General Motors, General Electric, and CBS to the *New York Times*, the New York City Board of Education, and the United Auto Workers."

Even academia, with its commitment to academic freedom, failed to fight McCarthyism. Nearly one-half of the social science professors teaching in universities at the time expressed medium or high apprehension about possible adverse repercussions to them as a result of their political beliefs and activities. In fact, Ellen Schrecker, in *No Ivory Tower: McCarthyism and the Universities*, found that academia contributed to McCarthyism. "The dismissals, the blacklists, and above all the almost universal acceptance of the legitimacy of what the congressional committees and other official investigators were doing conferred respectability upon the most repressive elements of the anticommunist crusade. In its collaboration with McCarthyism, the academic community behaved just like every other major institution in American life."

As Caute has shown, by 1949 twenty-two states required teachers to sign loyalty oaths as a condition of employment, twenty-one forbade "seditious" classroom instruction, and thirty-one considered membership in subversive organizations as defined by the Department of Justice a sufficient cause for dismissal. In California, twenty-eight public and private colleges, including Stanford University and the University of California at Berkeley, installed security officers—usually former FBI agents—to compile information on the political beliefs and affiliations of professors for state officials. Caute has calculated that as a consequence of these anticommunist laws and practices, more than 600 public school teachers and professors lost their jobs. Throughout the University of California system alone, twenty-six professors were dismissed who refused to sign the loyalty oath, thirty-seven others resigned in protest, forty-seven professors from other institutions turned down offers of appointment in California, and fifty-five courses from the university curriculum were eliminated. In *Compromised Campus: The Collaboration of Universities with the Intelligence Community*, Sigmund Desmond demonstrates that university officials, including the presidents of Yale and Harvard, secretly cooperated with the FBI while publicly portraying their institutions as bastions of academic freedom. Such draconian measures by the government and university administrators would trigger the "free speech movement" that began at the University of California, Berkeley, and activate students on campuses throughout the nation, leading to the rise of the New Left and antiwar movements.

Intimidation and Harassment

Perhaps most important, McCarthyism had a "chilling" effect throughout society; millions of Americans were intimidated by these repressive actions, for they sent clear messages to the public about what constituted proper political thought and behavior in American politics. As early as 1947 in response to the House Un-American Activities Committee's investigation of the Hollywood Ten—referring to ten top filmmakers and actors—Martha Gellhorn, a former leftist and one-time wife of Ernest Hemingway, sarcastically referred to it as "a little terror, calculated to frighten little people." But "it works"; under such pressure "a man can be well and truly destroyed." Her comments were prophetic. Someone "with a family will think many times before speaking his mind fearlessly and critically when there lies ahead the threat of an Un-Americans' investigation, a publicized branding, and his job gone." For if you could destroy the Hollywood Ten, "pretty soon you can ruin a painter and a teacher and a writer and a lawyer and an actor and a scientist; and presently you have made a silent place."

During this time the FBI maintained a widespread network of informants to weed out subversives and covertly instituted Operation COINTELPRO to target the Communist Party, USA. One of the "informants" was Ronald Reagan who, while serving as the president of the Screen Actors Guild, was secretly reporting to the FBI on suspect members of the union he was elected to represent. Under Director J. Edgar Hoover this counterintelligence program soon broadened to include the civil rights movement and then the antiwar movement during the 1960s.

The FBI ended up carrying out over 500,000 investigations of so-called subversives without a single court conviction and created files on over one million Americans. Hoover stated the goals of the activities of the "Disruption of the New Left" Internal Security Counter Intelligence Program to the FBI's Albany, New York, office in the following manner:

> The purpose of this program is to expose, disrupt, and otherwise neutralize the activities of the various new left organizations, their leadership and their adherents. It is impera-

tive that activities of those groups be followed on a continuous basis so we may take advantage of all opportunities for counter intelligence and also inspire action where circumstances warrant. . . . We must frustrate every effort of these groups and individuals to consolidate their forces or to recruit new or youthful adherents. In every instance, consideration should be given to disrupting organized activity of these groups and no opportunity should be missed to capitalize on organizational or personal conflicts of their leadership.

These steps, which violated the ability of Americans to exercise their liberties in accordance with the Constitution, were legitimate in the minds of Hoover and many American conservatives, for they believed that the civil rights movement and the New Left, including people like Martin Luther King, Jr., and Students for a Democratic Society leader Tom Hayden, were too radical, too un-American, and too threatening to the status quo, if not downright communist directed.

An Open Door for Covert Action

More moderate political leaders, including cold war liberals such as Lyndon B. Johnson and Hubert Humphrey, tended to support these counterintelligence actions because they were unsure about the influence of communism, their governmental legitimacy and power were being challenged, and they were repulsed by such nonconformist political behavior—especially since they were accustomed to a relatively politically supportive and passive population, especially when it came to foreign policy. As David Halberstam described LBJ's increasingly "bunker" mentality in the White House by 1966: "So instead of leading, he was immobilized, surrounded, seeing critics everywhere. Critics became enemies; enemies became traitors."

Although most Americans remained unaware of these covert actions at home, American nationalism believed in anticommunism and tolerated little dissent from the norm. This was, after all, the height of presidential power in exercising prerogative government in support of foreign policy in the name of national security. The right of political dissent and even a concern for public health were not allowed to get in the way of the war on communism—such was the primacy of the national security ethos throughout government.

For example, over 100,000 people who lived downwind from the Nevada Test Site felt the nuclear blasts and, more importantly, were exposed to the resulting radioactive fallout during the 1950s. These people were predominantly Mormons, very patriotic believers in God and country, who lived in small towns in Nevada and Utah. In addition, islanders have been exposed to radioactive fallout from nuclear tests in the Pacific; military troops have been exposed to radioactive fallout while engaged in war exercises following nuclear tests in the Pacific and the Nevada Test Site; civilians have been exposed to dangerous bacteria as a result of the army's germ warfare tests over populated areas; civilians were injected with radioactive substances in experiments to determine the effects of radiation; workers and local residents have been exposed to radiation from the government's nuclear weapons production facilities located throughout the country; miners and nearby residents have been exposed to radioactive material from uranium mines; Vietnam veterans (and countless local Vietnamese) have been exposed to dioxin in the chemical defoliant "Agent Orange"; and military personnel and civilians are exposed to military toxic wastes while they work and live near toxic waste dumps on military bases. Overall, it is estimated that millions of Americans, military and civilian, have been exposed to radioactive and toxic substances used by the U.S. government and the military in the name of national security.

Quelling Resistance

The politics of the cold war was serious business. Political instability was typically portrayed by supporters of the cold war and the Vietnam War as a function of communists or so-called "outside agitators" who were trying to stir up trouble. Cold war proponents simply could not understand that growing numbers of Americans were sincerely speaking out against them and their policies. Therefore, the FBI's programs were complemented by similar covert counterintelligence activities conducted throughout the national security bureaucracy. The Central Intelligence Agency opened the mail of American citizens, kept over 1.5 million names on file, and infiltrated religious, media, and academic groups. The National Security Agency monitored all cables sent overseas or received by Americans from 1947 to 1975. Army Intelligence investigated over 100,000 American citizens during the Vietnam War era. The Internal Revenue Service allowed tax information to be misused by intelligence agencies for political purposes.

The U.S. government, moreover, worked closely with local leaders, relying on the police and the National Guard, to prevent demonstrations and officially restore law and order. The criminal justice system, for example, was used to arrest, try, and, in some cases, convict demonstrators as a means of preventing and deterring the exercise of their civil liberties, thus producing "political prisoners." These efforts to repress dissent resulted in dozens of Americans being fatally shot by the police and the militia during the turbulent years of the 1960s, including four individuals at Kent State University in Ohio and two students at Jackson State University in Mississippi. Finally, President Nixon attempted to take things into his own hands by allowing White House operatives to destroy his enemies and guarantee the reelection of the president, leading to the Watergate crisis.

In almost every situation during the cold war years, the political dynamics were the same. The government and its conservative allies in virtually all levels of society resisted those who attempted to peacefully exercise their civil liberties through the political system and change the status quo from a liberal or leftist perspective. While the civil rights and antiwar movements were overwhelmingly involved in political acts of nonviolence and civil disobedience, among both leaders and followers, the government was engaged in a massive campaign to limit and stifle the exercise of civil rights and liberties. Acts by the police to disrupt demonstrations often resulted in violence, radicalization, increased repression, and more violence until American society seemed to be at war with itself. Ultimately, these efforts to restrict and neutralize the civil rights and liberties of Americans failed to contain the growth of massive political dissent against the Vietnam War during the 1960s and early 1970s. . . .

The End of the Cold War

With the collapse of the Soviet Union and communism in Eastern Europe, the end of the cold war has had important implications for the exercise of civil liberties and the future of American politics. First, Americans can rest assured that communism will likely have almost no appeal within the United States any longer. Therefore, Americans should have little reason to fear the threat of communism in the foreseeable future. Second, the decline of international communism means that anticommunism should fade as an important political issue (among liberals and especially conservatives), although the most extreme groups may continue to see the communist bogeyman on the march. In other words, where the threat of Bolshevism and communism has been used throughout the twentieth century by conservatives and the political Right to resist change and promote their policies, it should no longer have the symbolic value for uniting conservatives and attracting the support of Americans it had in the past, especially during the red scares of World War I and the cold war years.

The collapse of communism, in other words, has further expanded the ability of Americans to exercise their civil liberties in American politics. Americans can choose to participate in electoral and group politics with little fear for their civil liberties, personal standing, and livelihood, especially in comparison to the cold war years. This suggests that ideological diversity will continue to increase among the mass and elite public, while new foreign policy issues may generate more political involvement in electoral politics, social movements, and interest groups. This is probably best illustrated by the existence of a divided public and country before the actual initiation of hostilities in the Persian Gulf War. It also suggests the need and potential for the reduction, and possible reform, of the immense national security bureaucracy and the prevalence of the national security ethos.

However, even with the decline of communism, international conflict and new issues—such as drugs and terrorism—will continue to plague the world, bureaucratic institutions created to protect national security will continue to exist, and American nationalism will continue to promote conformity in response to crises. A type of dualism of freedom and intolerance with respect to the exercise of civil liberties has existed in the practice of American politics. On the one hand, American civil rights and liberties have steadily expanded throughout American history. In the post-Vietnam War era, Americans on the whole have become freer and more tolerant than during any previous period. This tolerance and freedom is much more in accordance with the ideals set down by the Declaration of Independence and the Constitution of the United States. On the other hand, there also have been periods of contraction in the exercise of civil liberties within the United States. Americans have been vulnerable to streaks of intolerance and discriminatory practices usually accompanied by emotional appeals to Americanism and nationalism, especially during times of war. These contradictory patterns in the exercise of civil liberties are reflected in the beliefs among both the mass and elite publics.

Americans Must Resist Senator McCarthy's Censorship

Edward R. Murrow

In the early 1950s few journalists dared to criticize the actions of Senator Joseph R. McCarthy, who led the anti-Communist witch hunts that ruined the careers of many artists, journalists, military officers, and government officials. The striking exception was Edward R. Murrow, a reporter who first gained distinction for his radio broadcasts during World War II. On March 9, 1954, Murrow and his coproducer, Fred Friendly, aired a thirty-minute exposé about McCarthy on their CBS news show, See It Now. CBS refused to publicly support or publicize the episode, and Murrow and Friendly had to use their own money to inform the public about the show. The exposé, presented in this selection, includes excerpts from McCarthy's own speeches to illustrate his contradictory statements and fanatical Red Scare tactics. It also profiles some of McCarthy's underhanded questioning of those brought before the Senate Permanent Subcommittee on Investigations in 1953 and 1954. By accusing those who disagreed with him of being Communist sympathizers, Senator McCarthy effectively censored dissent for many years. Murrow's powerful analysis of McCarthy contributed to the national outcry against the senator that eventually led to his downfall. McCarthy was investigated by a special Senate committee, and on December 2, 1954, the Senate voted to condem him for failing to cooperate with Senate investigations and for acting contrary to senatorial ethics. The Murrow report, along with televised reports of the McCarthy hearings, inspired a nationwide backlash against the Wisconsin senator. To this day, the broadcast is seen as a turning point in the history of television.

Edward R. Murrow, *See It Now*. New York: CBS-TV, 1954. Reproduced by permission.

Edward R. Murrow: Good evening. Tonight *See it Now* devotes its entire half hour to a report on Senator Joseph R. McCarthy told mainly in his own words and pictures. . . . Because a report on Senator [Joseph R.] McCarthy is by definition controversial we want to say exactly what we mean to say and I request your permission to read from the script whatever remarks Murrow and [producer Fred W.] Friendly may make. If the Senator believes we have done violence to his words or pictures and desires to speak, to answer himself, an opportunity will be afforded him on this program. Our working thesis tonight is this statement:

> If this fight against Communism is made a fight against America's two great political parties, the American people know that one of those parties will be destroyed and the Republic cannot endure very long as a one party system.

We applaud that statement and we think Senator McCarthy ought to. He said it, seventeen months ago in Milwaukee.

> *McCarthy*: The American people realize this cannot be made a fight between America's two great political parties. If this fight against Communism is made a fight between America's two great political parties the American people know that one of those parties will be destroyed and the Republic cannot endure very long as a one party system.

Murrow: Thus on February 4th, 1954, Senator McCarthy spoke of one party's treason. This was at Charleston, West Virginia, where there were no cameras running. It was recorded on tape.

> *McCarthy*: The issue between the Republicans and Democrats is clearly drawn. It has been deliberately drawn by those who have been in charge of twenty years of treason.
>
> The hard fact is—the hard fact is that those who wear the label, those who wear the label Democrat wear it with the stain of a historic betrayal.

Murrow: Seventeen months ago [presidential] Candidate [General Dwight D.] Eisenhower met Senator McCarthy in Green Bay, Wisconsin, and he laid down the ground rules on how he would meet Communism if elected.

> *Eisenhower*: This is a pledge I make. If I am charged by you people to be the responsible head of the Executive Department it will be my initial responsibility to see that subversion, disloyalty, is kept out of the Executive Department. We will always appreciate and welcome Congressional investigation but the responsibility will rest squarely on the shoulders of the Executive and I hold that there are ample powers in the government to get rid of these people if the Executive Department is really concerned in doing it. We can do it with absolute assurance. (Applause.)
>
> This is America's principle: Trial by jury, of the innocent until proved guilty, and I expect to stand to do it.

Murrow: That same night in Milwaukee, Senator McCarthy stated what he would do if [Eisenhower] General was elected.

> *McCarthy*: I spent about a half hour with the General last night. While I can't—while I can't report that we agreed entirely on everything—I can report that when I left that meeting with the General, I had the same feeling as when I went in, and that is that he is a great American, and will make a great President, an outstanding President. But I want to tell you tonight, tell the American people as long as I represent you and the rest of the American people in the Senate, I shall continue to call them as I see them regardless of who happens to be President.

Murrow: November 24th, 1953.

> *McCarthy*: A few days ago I read that President Eisenhower expressed the hope that by election time in 1954 the subject of Communism would be a dead and forgotten issue. The raw, harsh unpleasant fact is that Communism is an issue and will be an issue in 1954.

Murrow: On one thing the Senator has been consistent. . . . Often operating as a one-man committee, he has traveled far, interviewed many, terrorized some, accused civilian and military leaders of the past administration of a great conspiracy to turn the country over to Communism, investigated and substantially demoralized the present State Department, made varying charges of espionage at Fort Manmouth [Army Base]. (The Army says it has been unable to find anything relating to espionage there.) He has interrogated a varied assortment of what he calls "Fifth Amendment Communists." Republican Senator [Ralph] Flanders of Vermont said of McCarthy today:

> He dons war paint; he goes into his war dance; he emits his war whoops; he goes forth to battle and proudly returns with the scalp of a pink Army dentist.

Other critics have accused the Senator of using the bull whip and smear. There was a time two years ago when the Senator and his friends said he had been smeared and bull whipped.

> *Mr. Keefe*: You would sometimes think to hear the quartet that call themselves "Operation Truth" damning Joe McCarthy and resorting to the vilest smears I have ever heard. Well, this is the answer, and if I could express it in what is in my heart right now, I would do it in terms of the poet who once said:
>
> Ah 'tis but a dainty flower I bring
>   you,
> Yes, 'tis but a violet, glistening with
>   dew,
> But still in its heart there lies beau-
>   ties concealed
> So in our heart our love for you lies
>   unrevealed.

> *McCarthy*: You know, I used to pride myself on the idea that I was a bit tough, especially over the past eighteen or nineteen when we have been kicked around and bull

whipped and damned. I didn't think that I could be touched very deeply. But tonight, frankly, my cup and my heart is so full I can't talk to you.

Murrow: But in Philadelphia, on Washington's Birthday, 1954, his heart was so full he could talk. He reviewed some of the General [Ralph] Zwicker testimony and proved he hadn't abused him.

McCarthy: Nothing is more serious than a traitor to this country in the Communist conspiracy. Question: Do you think stealing $50 is more serious than being a traitor to the country and a part of the Communist conspiracy?

Answer: That, sir, was not my decision.

McCarthy: Shall we go on to that for a while? I hate to impose on your time. I just got two pages. This is the abuse which is ... the real meat of abuse, this is the official reporter's record of the hearing. After he said he wouldn't remove that General from the Army who cleared Communists, I said: "Then General, you should be removed from any Command. Any man who has been given the honor of being promoted to General, and who says, 'I will protect another general who protects Communists,' is not fit to wear that uniform, General." (Applause.)

I think it is a tremendous disgrace to the Army to have to bring these facts before the public but I intend to give it to the public, General. I have a duty to do that. I intend to repeat to the press exactly what you said so that you can know that and be back here to hear it, General.

And wait till you hear the bleeding hearts scream and cry about our methods of trying to drag the truth from those who know, or should know, who covered up a Fifth Amendment Communist Major. But they say, 'Oh, it's all right to uncover them but don't get rough doing it, McCarthy.'

Murrow: But two days later, Secretary [Robert T.] Stevens and the Senator had lunch, agreed on a memorandum of understanding, and disagreed on what the small type said.

Stevens: I shall never accede to the abuse of Army personnel under any circumstance including committee hearings. I shall not accede to them being brow-beaten or humiliated. In the light of these assurances, although I did not propose cancellation of the hearings, I acceded to it. If it had not been for these assurances, I would never have entered into any agreement whatsoever.

Murrow: Then President Eisenhower issued a statement that advisers thought censored the Senator, but the Senator saw it as another victory, called the entire Zwicker case "a tempest in a teapot."

McCarthy: If a stupid, arrogant or witless man in a position of power appears before our Committee and is found aiding the Communist Party, he will be exposed. The fact that he might be a General places him in no special class as far as I am concerned. Apparently—apparently, the President and I now agree on the necessity of getting rid of Communists. We apparently disagree on how we should handle those who protect Communists. When the shouting and the tumult dies, the American people and the President will realize that this unprecedented mud slinging against the Committee by the extreme left wing elements of press and radio was caused solely because another Fifth Amendment Communist was finally dug out of the dark recesses and exposed to the public view.

Murrow (points to a chart): Senator McCarthy claims that only the left wing press criticized him on the Zwicker case. Of the fifty large circulation newspapers in the country, these are the left wing papers that criticized. These are the ones which supported him. The ratio is about three to one against the Senator. Now let us look at some of these left wing papers that criticized the Senator.

The Chicago Tribune: McCarthy will better serve his cause if he learns to distinguish the role of investigator from role of avenging angel . . .

The New York Times: The unwarranted interference of a demagogue—a domestic Munich . . .

The Times Herald, Washington: Senator McCarthy's behavior towards Zwicker is not justified . . .

The Herald Tribune of New York: McCarthyism involves assaults on basic Republican concepts . . .

Milwaukee Journal: The line must be drawn and defended or McCarthy will become the government . . .

The Evening Star of Washington: It was a bad day for everyone who resents and detests the bully boy tactics which Senator McCarthy often employs . . .

The New York World Telegram: Bamboozling, bludgeoning, distorting . . .

St. Louis Post Dispatch: Unscrupulous, McCarthy bullying. What a tragic irony it is that the President's political advisors keep him from doing what every decent instinct must be commanding him to do . . .

Well, that's the ratio of a three-to-one, so-called "left-wing" press.

Another interesting thing was said about the Zwicker case, and it was said by Senator McCarthy.

McCarthy: Well, may I say that I was extremely shocked when I heard that Secretary Stevens told two Army officers that they had to take part in the cover-up of those who promoted and coddled Communists. As I read his statement, I thought of that quotation "On what meat doth this, our Caesar, feed?"[1]

Murrow: And upon what meat doth Senator McCarthy feed? Two of the staples of his diet are the investigation (protected by immunity) and the half-truth. We herewith submit samples of both.

1. A quote from William Shakespeare's play *Julius Caesar*.

First, the half-truth. This was an attack on [presidential candidate] Adlai Stevenson at the end of the 1952 campaign. President Eisenhower, it must be said, had no prior knowledge of it.

McCarthy: I perform this unpleasant task because the American people are entitled to have the coldly documented history of this man who says, "I want to be your President."

Strangely, Alger—I mean, Adlai [laughter]—But let's move on to another part of the jigsaw puzzle. Now, while you think—while you may think there can be no connection between the debonair Democratic candidate and a dilapidated Massachusetts barn, I want to show you a picture of this barn and explain the connection.

Here is the outside of the barn. Give me the pictures of the inside, if you will. Here is the outside of the barn up at Lee, Massachusetts. It looks as though it couldn't house a farmer's cow or goat from the outside. Here's the inside: a beautifully panelled conference room with maps of the Soviet Union. Well, in what way does Stevenson tie up with that?

My—my investigators went out and took pictures of the barn after we had been tipped off of what was in it—tipped off that there was in this barn all the missing documents from the Communist front—IPR—the IPR which has been named by the McCarran Committee—named before the McCarran Committee as a coverup for Communist espionage.[2]

Now, let's take a look at a photostat of a document taken from the Massachusetts barn—one of those documents which was never supposed to see the light of day. Rather interesting it is. This is a document which shows that Alger Hiss and Frank Coe [alleged Soviet spies] recommended Adlai Stevenson to the Mount Tremblant Conference which was called for the purpose of establishing for-

2. The "McCarran Committee" was the Senate Internal Security Subcommitte chaired by Nevada Senator Pat McCarran. The committee investigated educational institutions trade unions, and federal offices to root out so-called "subversive activities." Senator McCarran came to be known for using intimidation and harassment against uncooperative witnesses.

eign policy (postwar foreign policy) in Asia. And, as you know, Alger Hiss is a convicted traitor. Frank Coe has been named under oath before congressional committees seven times as a member of the Communist Party. Why? Why do Hiss and Coe find that Adlai Stevenson is the man they want representing them at this conference? I don't know. Perhaps Adlai knows.

Murrow: But Senator McCarthy didn't permit his audience to hear the entire paragraph. This is the official record of the McCarran hearings. Anyone can buy it for two dollars. Here's a quote: "Another possibility for the Mount Tremblant conferences on Asia is someone from Knox' office or Stimson's office." (Frank Knox was our wartime Secretary of the Navy; Henry Stimson our Secretary of the Army, both distinguished Republicans.) And it goes on: "Coe, and Hiss mentioned Adlai Stevenson (one of Knox' special assistants) and Harvey Bundy (former Assistant Secretary of State under Hoover, and now assistant to Stimson) because of their jobs."

We read from this documented record, not in defense of Mr. Stevenson, but in defense of truth. Specifically, Mr. Stevenson's identification with that red barn was no more, no less than that of Knox, Stimson or Bundy. It should be stated that Mr. Stevenson was once a member of the Institute of Pacific Relations. But so were such other loyal Americans as Senator Ferguson, John Foster Dulles, Paul Hoffman, Harry Luce and Herbert Hoover. Their association carries with it no guilt, and that barn has nothing to do with any of them.

Now—a sample investigation. The witness was Reed Harris, for many years a civil servant in the State Department, directing the information service. Harris was accused of helping the Communistic cause by curtailing some broadcasts to Israel. Senator McCarthy summoned him and questioned him about a book he had written in 1932.

McCarthy: Now we'll come to order. Mr. Reed Harris? Your name is Reed Harris?

Harris: That's correct.

McCarthy: You wrote a book in '32, is that correct?

Harris: Yes, I wrote a book. As I testified in executive session . . .

McCarthy: At the time you wrote the book—pardon me; go ahead. I'm sorry. Proceed.

Harris: At the time I wrote the book the atmosphere in the universities of the United States was greatly affected by the great depression then in existence. The attitudes of students, the attitudes of the general public were considerably different than they are at this moment and for one thing there was generally no awareness, to the degree that there is today, of the way the Communist Party works.

McCarthy: You attended Columbia University in the early thirties. Is that right?

Harris: I did, Mr. Chairman.

McCarthy: Will you speak a little louder, sir?

Harris: I did, Mr. Chairman.

McCarthy: And were you expelled from Columbia?

Harris: I was suspended from classes on April 1st, 1932. I was later reinstated and I resigned from the University.

McCarthy: And you resigned from the University? Did the Civil—Civil Liberties Union provide you with an attorney at that time?

Harris: I had many offers of attorneys, and one of those was from the American Civil Liberties Union, yes.

McCarthy: The question is did the Civil Liberties Union supply you with an attorney?

Harris: They did supply an attorney.

McCarthy: The answer is yes?

Harris: The answer is yes.

McCarthy: You know the Civil Liberties Union has been listed as "a front for, and doing the work of," the Communist Party?

Harris: Mr. Chairman this was 1932.

McCarthy: Yeah, I know it was 1932. Do you know that they since have been listed as "a front for, and doing the work of" the Communist Party?

Harris: I do not know that they have been listed so, sir.

McCarthy: You don't know they have been listed?

Harris: I have heard that mentioned or read that mentioned.

McCarthy: Now, you wrote a book in 1932. I'm going to ask you again: at the time you wrote this book, did you feel that professors should be given the right to teach sophomores that marriage—and I quote—"should be cast out of our civilization as antiquated and stupid religious phenomena?" Was that your feeling at that time?

Harris: My feeling is that professors should have the right to express their considered opinions on any subject, whatever they were, sir.

McCarthy: All right, I'm going to ask you this question again.

Harris: That includes that quotation. They should have the right to teach anything that came into their minds as being the proper thing to teach.

McCarthy: I'm going to make you answer this.

Harris: All right, I'll answer yes, but you put an implication on it and you feature this particular point of the book, which, of course, is quite out of context, does not give a proper impression of the book as a whole. The American public doesn't get an honest impression of even that book, bad as it is, from what you are quoting from it.

McCarthy: Well, then, let's continue to read your own writing, and . . .

Harris: Twenty-one years ago, again.

McCarthy: Yes, but we shall try and bring you down to date, if we can.

Harris: Mr. Chairman, two weeks ago, Senator [Robert A.] Taft took the position that I took twenty-one years ago, that Communists and Socialists should be allowed to teach in the schools. It so happens that, nowadays I don't agree with Senator Taft, as far as Communist teaching in the schools is concerned, because I think Communists are, in effect, a plainclothes auxiliary of the Red Army, the Soviet Red Army. And I don't want to see them in any of our schools, teaching.

McCarthy: I don't recall Senator Taft ever having any of the background that you've got, sir.

Harris: I resent the tone of this inquiry very much, Mr. Chairman. I resent it, not only because it is my neck, my public neck, that you are, I think, very skillfully trying to wring, but I say it because there are thousands of able and loyal employees in the federal government of the United States who have been properly cleared according to the laws and the security practices of their agencies, as I was—unless the new regime says no; I was before.

[Senator John L.] McClellan: Do you think this book did considerable harm, its publication might have had adverse influence on the public by an expression of views contained in it?

Harris: The sale of that book was so abysmally small. It was so unsuccessful that a question of its influence. . . . Really, you can go back to the publisher. You'll see it was one of the most unsuccessful books he ever put out. He's still sorry about it, just as I am.

McClellan: Well, I think that's a compliment to American intelligence. (laughter). I will say that for him.

Murrow: Senator McCarthy succeeded in proving that Reed Harris had once written a bad book, which the American people had proved twenty-two years ago by not buying it, which is what they eventually do with all bad ideas. As for Reed Harris, his resignation was accepted a month later with a letter of commendation. McCarthy claimed it as a victory.

The Reed Harris hearing demonstrates one of the Senator's techniques. Twice he said the American Civil Liberties Union was listed as a subversive front. The Attorney General's list does not and has never listed the ACLU as subversive, nor does the FBI or any other federal government agency. And the American Civil Liberties Union holds in its files letters of commendation from President [Harry S.] Truman, President Eisenhower, and General [Douglas] MacArthur.

Now let us try to bring the McCarthy story a little more up to date. Two years ago Senator Benton of Connecticut accused McCarthy of apparent perjury, unethical practice, and perpetrating a hoax on the Senate. McCarthy sued for two million dollars. Last week he dropped the case, saying no one could be found who believed Benton's story. Several volunteers have come forward saying they believe it in its entirety.

Today Senator McCarthy says he's going to get a lawyer and force the networks to give him time to reply to Adlai Stevenson's speech.

Earlier, the Senator asked, "Upon what meat does this, our Caesar, feed?" Had he looked three lines earlier in Shakespeare's Caesar, he would have found this line, which is not altogether inappropriate: "The fault, dear Brutus, is not in our stars, but in ourselves."

No one familiar with the history of this country can deny that congressional committees are useful. It is necessary to investigate before legislating, but the line between investigating and persecuting is a very fine one and the junior Senator from Wisconsin has stepped over it repeatedly. His primary achievement has been in confusing the public mind, as between the internal and the external threats of Communism. We must not confuse dissent with disloyalty. We must remember always that accusation is not proof and that conviction depends upon evidence and due process of law. We will not walk in fear, one of another. We will not be driven by fear into an age of unreason, if we dig deep in our history and our doctrine, and remember that we are not descended from fearful men—not from men who feared to write, to speak, to associate and to defend causes that were, for the moment, unpopular.

This is no time for men who oppose Senator McCarthy's methods to keep silent, or for those who approve. We can deny our heritage and our history, but we cannot escape responsibility for the result. There is no way for a citizen of a republic to abdicate his responsibilities. As a nation we have come into our full inheritance at a tender age. We proclaim ourselves, as indeed we are, the defenders of freedom, wherever it continues to exist in the world, but we cannot defend freedom abroad by deserting it at home.

The actions of the junior Senator from Wisconsin have caused alarm and dismay amongst our allies abroad, and given considerable comfort to our enemies. And whose fault is that? Not really his. He didn't create this situation of fear; he merely exploited it—and rather successfully. Cassius was right. "The fault, dear Brutus, is not in our stars, but in ourselves."

Good night, and good luck.

A Landmark Case over the Censorship of Films

Marjorie Heins

When motion pictures were invented in the early twentieth century, they introduced a powerful form of artistic expression and became an extremely lucrative American industry. It is not surprising, then, that the cinema also has a long history of censorship struggles. In this selection Marjorie Heins chronicles the saga of The Miracle, *an Italian film that provoked extreme resistance from the Catholic Church leadership and some Catholic citizen groups when it was brought to U.S. theaters in 1950. Critics of the film claimed that it was blasphemous because it sympathetically portrays a woman who mistakenly believes her pregnancy to be an immaculate conception. As Heins explains, religious institutions, and particularly the Catholic Church, have played a major role in the regulation of cinema in the United States. The legal uproar over* The Miracle *convinced the New York City license commissioner to pull the film from New York theaters, and subsequently the film's American distributor filed a lawsuit to challenge the action. In 1952, the legal case over* The Miracle *went all the way to the Supreme Court, which ruled unanimously that government censorship of films based on sacrilege is unconstitutional. However, to maintain the loyalty of religious moviegoers and avoid costly legal suits in the future, leaders in the film industry decided to regulate Hollywood movies under the auspices of the Motion Picture Association of America's Production Code, which strictly controlled the content of films. The stringent code lost favor in the 1960s and was replaced by a ratings system that is still in effect today.*

Marjorie Heins, "The Miracle: Film Censorship and the Entanglement of Church and State," *Forum for Contemporary Thought*, October 6, 2003. Reproduced by permission. The full text of the speech, with citations to sources, can be found at http://www.fepproject.org/commentaries/themiracle.html.

Marjorie Heins is the founder of the Free Expression Policy Project at the New York University School of Law and the author of numerous books about freedom of expression, including Not in Front of the Children: "Indecency," Censorship, and the Innocence of Youth.

[Editor's Note: The following selection is an extract of a lecture Marjorie Heins delivered to the Forum for Contemporary Thought on October 28, 2002.]

My topic today is one of the most important art censorship cases in U.S. history. It began in 1951 with a ban on a short film called *The Miracle*, by the Italian neorealist master, Roberto Rossellini, and ended in a monumental Supreme Court decision. The case also raised profound questions about the separation of church and state, questions that still bedevil our society today.

Let me give you an overview of the case; afterwards, I'll talk in more detail about the history of film censorship, the pivotal role of the Catholic Church, and some of the lessons of the *Miracle* case.

Late in December 1950, Rossellini's *Il Miracolo* opened at the Paris Theater in Manhattan. The film is a religious parable featuring a dim-witted peasant woman, Nanni (played brilliantly by Anna Magnani), who is plied with drink and then seduced by a vagabond whom she mistakes in her stupor for St. Joseph. (St. Joseph is played by the young Federico Fellini, who also wrote the screenplay.)

It's not clear whether Nanni is even awake for the actual sex, but in any event, she soon discovers she is pregnant and decides it is an immaculate conception. Her fellow villagers are not so naive; they mock and torment her, even singing religious hymns as they parade her through the streets with a basin instead of a halo on her head. Nanni escapes to a hilltop church, and experiences a beatific moment of religious ecstasy after giving birth alone on the church floor.

Early Criticism and Censorship of *The Miracle*

When released in Italy in 1948, *The Miracle* was harshly criticized by the Catholic Cinematographic Center—an arm of the Vatican devoted to vetting movies for moral propriety. But it was not banned—indeed, it was shown at the Venice Film Festival, where works considered blasphemous by the Vatican would not have been allowed. The Vatican's semi-official newspaper, *Osservatore Romano*, published a guardedly appreciative review, noting that "objections from a religious viewpoint are very grave," but also pointing to "scenes of undoubted screen value," and concluding that "we still believe in Rossellini's art."

In New York City, public officials were not so broadminded. City License Commissioner Edward McCaffrey, a former state commander of the Catholic War Veterans, announced that he found *The Miracle* "officially and personally blasphemous," and ordered the manager of the Paris [theater] to stop showing it. The next day, the Catholic Church's Legion of Decency called *The Miracle* a "blasphemous mockery of Christian-religious truth," and McCaffrey suspended the theater's license.

The film's distributor, Joseph Burstyn, filed a lawsuit to challenge McCaffrey. Burstyn was a champion of foreign films; several years earlier, he had introduced Americans to the glories of post-World War II European cinema by exhibiting Rossellini's masterpiece, *Open City*. Movie star Ingrid Bergman, bored by performing in formulaic Hollywood vehicles, was entranced by *Open City* when she saw it, and by Rossellini's next feature, *Paisan*. Whereupon she sent Rossellini one of the more famous letters in cinema history. "I am ready to come and make a film with you," Bergman wrote, "even though I know only two words in Italian: '*Ti amo*' [I love you]." With this introduction, it was probably only a matter of time before Bergman deserted her husband and ran off with Rossellini. The affair was still good tabloid copy when *The*

Miracle opened at the Paris in Manhattan as part of a trilogy of short foreign films called *The Ways of Love.*

Burstyn's lawsuit came before a judge who, at a preliminary hearing, questioned McCaffrey's power to censor movies. Film censorship was well-entrenched in New York, but it was vested in the state Board of Regents, not the municipal license commissioner. Exhibitors had to apply in advance to the state board before showing any film. McCaffrey backed off and lifted his ban.

Protests and Picketing

But now a more powerful figure, Francis Cardinal Spellman, entered the fray, with a statement attacking *The Miracle* that he ordered read at every mass in all 400 parishes of the huge New York Archdiocese. Spellman, a right-winger whose political power was such that he was known as the "American Pope," had not seen *The Miracle*, but he had heard about it. This was enough for him to condemn the film as "a despicable affront to every Christian" and "a vicious insult to Italian womanhood" which should really be named "'Woman Further Defamed,' by Roberto Rossellini" (a reference, of course, to the affair with Bergman). Spellman said it was "a blot upon the escutcheon of the Empire State that no means of appeal to the Board of Regents is available to the people for the correcting of the mistake made by its motion picture division" in giving a license to exhibit *The Miracle* in the first place.

Picketing began at the Paris the same day, and continued for several weeks. Sometimes numbering more than 1,000, these representatives of the Catholic War Veterans, Knights of Columbus, and Archdiocesan Union of the Holy Name Society carried signs bearing such messages as: "This Picture is an Insult to Every Decent Woman and Her Mother," "This Picture is Blasphemous," and "Don't be a Communist—all the Communists are inside." They yelled similar affronts: "Don't enter that cesspool!", "Buy American!", "Don't look at that filth!"

Eight days after Cardinal Spellman's lament that there was no way for the state to rectify its error in licensing *The Miracle*, a way was found. A three-man committee of the Board of Regents convened, viewed the film, and declared it "sacrilegious." Four days later, the full Board directed Burstyn to "show cause" why the exhibition license should not be withdrawn. And on February 15, 1951, despite briefs supporting artistic freedom from the Authors League, prominent Protestant clergy, the ACLU, and assorted writers and intellectuals, the full Board ruled that the film was sacrilegious and therefore in violation of New York's 30-year-old film censorship law. *The Miracle* parodied the Immaculate Conception and Virgin Birth, they explained, "—concepts sacred to [millions of our people]," and inexcusably associated them with "drunkenness, seduction, mockery and lewdness."

Church and State: Separate or Not?

Burstyn's attorney, the First Amendment expert Ephraim London, now took an appeal; but the state courts rejected his arguments that not only the sacrilege standard, but the very existence of movie licensing, violated the First Amendment. On the contrary, using a rationale that is often heard today from those advocating state benefits for religion, the New York judges said they were simply accommodating citizens' religious preferences. *Not* to protect believers against "gratuitous insult" to their religious beliefs, according to the state Court of Appeals' logic, would amount to discrimination against them and hence an infringement of their freedom "to worship and believe as they choose."

The appeals court disposed of arguments by both London and the American Jewish Congress (in a friend-of-the-court brief) that the Church-driven censorship of *The Miracle* violated the First Amendment's Establishment Clause, which prohibits Congress from making any "law respecting an establishment of religion," and is generally understood to mandate the separation of church and state. The state's obeisance to Cardinal Spellman yielded only an "incidental" benefit to religion, said the court; and in any event, "[w]e are essentially a religious nation, . . . of which it is well to be reminded now and then."

London now appealed to the Supreme Court; and in a unanimous decision in May 1952 in the case of *Burstyn v. Wilson*, the Court declared "sacrilege" far too vague a censorship standard to be permitted under the First Amendment. Weaving an elaborate metaphor, Justice Tom Clark wrote for the Court that trying to decide what qualifies as sacrilege sets the censor "adrift upon a boundless sea amid a myriad of conflicting currents of religious views, with no charts but those provided by the most vocal and powerful orthodoxies." He added that "it is not the business of government . . . to suppress real or imagined attacks upon a particular religious doctrine."

Clark noted in passing that banning films because of sacrilege might also "raise substantial questions" under the Establishment Clause; indeed, censorship based on a standard like "sacrilege" inevitably favors vocal and powerful religions over quieter and weaker ones. "Under such a standard, the most careful and tolerant censor would find it virtually impossible to avoid favoring one religion over another."

But Clark stopped short of deciding the case on Establishment Clause grounds—with consequences that reverberate today. With government vouchers funding religious schools, a White House Office of Faith-Based Initiatives, and widespread outrage last summer [2002] over a federal court decision recognizing that the words "under God" in the Pledge of Allegiance represent government endorsement of religion, we are still wrestling with the issues in the *Miracle* case.

Religion and Film Censorship in America

Let's go back now to the beginning of film censorship in America and trace the role of religious institutions. In the early 1900s, Progressive Era Protestant reformers joined with more conservative clergy in alarm over the new, cheap "nickelodeon" theaters that were popular with urban adolescents and the working class. The nickelodeons featured short films of vaudeville-inspired melodrama and burlesque, bawdy street scenes (for example, breezes exposing women's underclothes), and crime stories like *The Great Train Robbery* (1903), America's first big cinematic hit. Early filmmakers also "turned to popular literature [and] drama," as historian Gregory Black recounts; they explored "'the corruption of city politics, the scandal of white slave rackets, the exploitation of immigrants' . . .; [they] 'championed the cause of labor, lobbied against political 'bosses,' and often gave dignity to the struggles of the urban poor.'"

But neither the social themes nor the artistry of early American cinema mitigated the concerns of the Progressive Era's anti-vice crusaders. In the words of film scholar Garth Jowett, reformers accused the nickelodeons of causing "every conceivable social ill, from sexual license to demonstrating the arts of pickpocketing to fomenting social revolution."

Municipalities and states quickly responded with censorship laws. Chicago led the way in 1907, with an ordinance that required exhibitors to secure a permit from the police before showing any film. Pennsylvania followed in 1911, Kansas and Ohio in 1913, Maryland in 1916. New York established a motion picture commission in 1921, directed to deny exhibition licenses to any film it considered "obscene, indecent, immoral, inhuman, sacrilegious, or . . . of such character that its exhibition would tend to corrupt morals or incite to crime." With little change, this was the law at issue in the *Miracle* case.

Are Movies Art or Business—or Both?

A legal challenge to the new licensing restrictions was inevitable; it reached the Supreme Court in 1915. The Mutual Film Company claimed that Ohio's film censorship law violated both the First Amendment and a similar provision in the state Constitution. But the Court, in a decision that shocked the nascent film industry, upheld the licensing scheme, ruling that cinema was not a form of expression protected by the First Amendment.

The exhibition of movies "is a business, pure and simple," said the Court. Movies are "originated and conducted for profit, like other spectacles [such as circuses, and are] not to be regarded . . . as part of the press of the country, or as organs of public opinion." Certainly, movies communicate ideas, the Court acknowledged; but censorship was justified because of the nature of movie audiences and the medium's capacity for "evil" and potential appeal to "prurient interest."

The subtext here was difficult to miss. As Garth Jowett writes, books and newspapers were also sold for profit, but not subject to prior-restraint licensing. The assertion that cinema has greater "capacity for evil" was based "on the presumed susceptibility of its 'primary audience . . . largely the immigrant working class.'"

The *Mutual Film* decision gave the green light to film censorship, and in the 50 years that followed, thousands of movies were cut, bowdlerized, or outright banned by state and local censors. Chicago banned newsreels of policemen shooting labor pickets; "ordered the deletion of a scene depicting the birth of a buffalo in Walt Disney's *Vanishing Prairie*"; refused a license for *Anatomy of a Murder*, "because it found the use of the words 'rape' and 'contraceptive' to be objectionable"; and banned Charlie Chaplin's classic satiric attack on Hitler, *The Great Dictator*, "apparently out of deference to its large German population." Atlanta banned *Lost Boundaries*, the story of "a Negro doctor's attempt to pass as white," on the ground that it would "adversely affect the peace, morals, and good order" of the city. A film version of *Carmen* was condemned in Ohio because girls "smoked cigarettes in public," and in Pennsylvania because of "the duration of a kiss." In

1928 alone, writes Black, New York's censorship board "cut over 4,000 scenes from the more than 600 films submitted, and Chicago censors sliced more than 600 scenes."

This highly decentralized system left much to be desired from the viewpoint of both Catholic and Protestant critics, as well as anti-vice crusaders like the Women's Christian Temperance Union (the WCTU), and indeed, the industry itself. For one thing, not all states and localities had censorship boards. (By 1922, seven states and about 100 localities did.) For another, their standards varied widely. While Protestant clergy and moral reformers were outraged at sexual content (Cecil B. DeMille's orgiastic biblical epics were a particular concern), Southern cities banned anything even remotely provocative on the subject of race.

The Hollywood Production Code

As more licensing bills were introduced in state legislatures (about 100 were considered in 1921 alone), and reformers pushed for a uniform national censorship system, Hollywood took its first stab at improving its image and thereby, it hoped, stopping the legislative juggernaut. In 1922, the major studios formed the Motion Picture Producers & Distributors of America (MPPDA) and hired Will Hays, former Postmaster General and head of the Republican National Committee, as its director. "Teetotaler, elder in the Presbyterian Church, Elk, Moose, Rotarian, and Mason," as Black writes, "Hays brought the respectability of mainstream middle America to a Jewish-dominated film industry."

Hays introduced a list of "Don'ts and Be Carefuls" for movies. Among the many disapproved subjects were profanity, nudity, "illegal traffic in drugs," white slavery, miscegenation, "sex hygiene and venereal diseases," scenes of childbirth, and "ridicule of the clergy." But the studios interpreted this pre-Code as they chose, and bridled at Hays's efforts to control them. Dissatisfied, Protestant clergy continued to press for a national censorship law. One Protestant minister, William

Chase, for example, complained in 1921 that the industry's "Hebrew" owners were "vile corrupters of American morals," and a "threat to world civilization." This anti-Semitism, not always so blatant but always lurking beneath the surface, would be a continuing theme as activists pressed for greater film censorship.

The Catholic Church now began to organize. The major strategist was Martin Quigley, a Chicago publisher of an industry trade journal who favored censorship but not by municipal licensing authorities, which had shown themselves all too amenable to payoffs. Quigley saw that more effective control of movie content could be achieved through vetting and editing at the pre-production stage. He persuaded Chicago's Cardinal George Mundelein and a Jesuit priest, FitzGeorge Dinneen, to develop a Catholic code for movies. In 1929, they invited a young Jesuit theologian named Daniel Lord to help them draft such a code.

Lord's draft not only contained specific prohibitions but announced sweeping moral prescriptions—for example, the general principle that no film should "lower the moral standards of those who see it. Hence the sympathy of the audience should never be thrown to the side of crime, wrongdoing, evil or sin." "Impure love" should not be presented so as "to arouse passion"; nudity or semi-nudity should never be shown, nor should "lustful kissing." Government and organized religion should not be disparaged, nor should ministers be comic characters or villains.

Lord's code came at an opportune time for Will Hays. With the movie industry in jitters after the recent stock market crash, with the Church's threat of 20 million Catholics boycotting immoral movies, and perhaps most important, with investment bankers—on whom the new, expensive "talkies" depended for financing—sounding the alarm to studio boards, Hays persuaded the producers to accept Father Lord's draft, and in 1930, with only minor changes, it became the Hollywood Production Code.

Between 1930 and '34, Hays and his staff struggled with Hollywood's producers to enforce the Code. But if anything, movies got saltier in the early 1930s, as studios labored to attract audiences despite the Depression. Mae West's *She Done Him Wrong*, with its sexy banter and hip-rolling heroine, was a hit in 1932; her *I'm No Angel* the following year was equally egregious, and popular with Americans of both sexes. The great gangster films—*Little Caesar, Scarface, Public Enemy*—were all produced in the early '30s when Lord's Code was supposedly in effect. Cecil B. DeMille's Roman orgies continued to succeed at the box office and outrage the Church.

The Production Code Administration

Frustrated by this state of affairs, Quigley and several prominent American bishops persuaded Monsignor Amleto Cicognani, visiting from the Vatican in 1934, to urge harsher action against Hollywood. Cicognani's subsequent speech to Catholic Charities in New York mourned the movies' "massacre of innocence of youth" and urged Catholics to unite in a campaign "for the purification of the cinema." With this seeming imperative from Rome, the U.S. Conference of Catholic Bishops now vowed to create a "Legion of Decency" that would decide which movies should be forbidden to Catholics, and to organize boycotts of theaters that showed any film thus condemned.

Hays welcomed the pressure. Like the Church, he preferred industry self-regulation to government censorship. Bolstered by the threats from bankers, Hays now established the Production Code Administration (PCA) to vet all scripts in advance, and hired Joseph Breen, a brash PR man and unrepentant anti-Semite who had worked with Martin Quigley in Chicago, to head the new censorship office.

Breen had already expressed frustration at the producers' independence. In 1932, he wrote to Father Wilfred Parsons, a fellow censorship activist and a Jesuit professor, that Hays was wrong to think "these lousy Jews out here [in Hollywood] would abide by the Code's provisions." Hays lacked "proper knowledge of the breed," Breen continued. ". . . They are simply a rotten bunch of vile people with no respect for anything beyond the making of money." There is no record that Father Parsons or any other church official took Breen to task for these and similar comments.

By the late 1930s, between the Legion of Decency in New York and Breen, the Church's delegate at the PCA in Hollywood, the Catholic Church controlled the content of American movies. Every script was submitted in advance, and if rejected, was rewritten to conform to Breen's requirements. In 1936, his office reviewed over 1,200 of them, and had more than 1,400 conferences with producers and directors to discuss rewrites. And if, after this laborious process, Legion of Decency headquarters in New York still objected to certain dialogue or scenes, Breen would force further changes. Thus in 1941 when the Legion disapproved of a Greta Garbo comedy, *Two-Faced Woman*, because of its "un-Christian attitude toward marriage," and Cardinal Spellman pronounced the film "dangerous to public morality," MGM withdrew it, then added scenes to negate any hint of adultery.

This isn't to say, of course, that Hollywood's output from 1934 until the gradual weakening of the Production Code in the 1950s consisted only of mom, apple pie, and moralizing. Producers were adept at suggesting events that couldn't be shown directly. Crime, evil, and fallen women were timeless themes; and as long as sin was punished in the end, a moralizing voiceover penned by Breen would usually suffice to qualify the film for PCA approval. In addition, rebel producers occasionally won small victories, such as David O. Selznick's famous refusal in 1939 to delete Rhett Butler's "frankly, my dear, I don't give a damn" from *Gone With the Wind*. But overall, the system was tightly controlled by the

Hays Office, with the Legion often forcing even more changes after Breen had finished tinkering.

Foreign Films Threaten Church Control

In 1950, the Legion of Decency's annual report noted with dismay that foreign films were gaining popularity in America. And the Legion had judged 53% of them to be objectionable either "wholly or in part."

Rossellini's *Open City* was typical. This 1945 classic depicts the Nazi occupation of Rome during the last months of the World War II. With its gritty realism, suggestions of lesbianism, horrifying scenes of Nazi torture, and powerful performance by Anna Magnani as Pina, a working class woman pregnant without benefit of marriage, who is savagely shot down in the film's most famous scene, *Open City* was a definite change from sanitized Hollywood fare. Based on the true story of an Italian priest who had been executed for helping the Resistance, *Open City* contained a hint of things to come when the evil Nazi commander asks the priest why he aids subversives and atheists, and the good father responds: "I am a Catholic priest and I believe that a man who fights for justice and liberty walks in the pathways of the Lord—and the pathways of the Lord are infinite."

Open City grossed an amazing (for a foreign film) $3 million at the U.S. box office and was chosen Best Film of 1946 by the New York Film Critics. Audiences in New York and Los Angeles loved it. (We already know how Ingrid Bergman reacted.) But with the U.S. Catholic Church still angry at the adulterous pair, Rossellini could expect little mercy from Cardinal Spellman when his next expression of egalitarian spirituality opened in New York in December 1950.

Support for *The Miracle*

Not all Catholics agreed with Spellman's attack on *The Miracle*. By mid-1951, a number of prominent Catholic intellectuals had protested the Church's position. As Otto Spaeth, director of the American Federation of Arts, wrote: "There was indeed 'blasphemy'" in *The Miracle*, "but it was the blasphemy of the villagers, who stopped at nothing, not even the mock singing of a hymn to the Virgin, in their brutal badgering of the tragic woman."

Similarly, *Commonweal* magazine editorialized: "sometimes it seems as if we American Catholics reduce the struggle for the hearts and minds of men to a contest between picket lines and pressure groups and in doing so slight the emphasis Catholic doctrine puts on free consent and reasoned morality." Two weeks later, an article by Notre Dame professor William Clancy in *Commonweal* reported that many prominent Catholics had found *The Miracle* "deeply moving" and "profoundly religious." Clancy essayed that Catholic campaigns against movies shocked "many loyal Catholics," who were "profoundly disturbed to see certain of our co-religionists embarked upon crusades which we feel can result only in great harm to the cause of religion, of art, and of intelligence."

Even the idiosyncratically religious Rossellini wrote to Spellman, explaining his spiritual intentions in the film. "In *The Miracle*, men are still without pity because they have not gone back to God," the director explained:

> But God is already present in the faith, however confused, of the poor persecuted woman and since God is forever, a human being suffers and is misunderstood. "The Miracle" occurs when, with the birth of the child, the poor demented woman regains sanity in her maternal love. They were my intentions and I hope that your Eminence will deign to consider them with paternal benevolence.

The Supreme Court Case

As the case made its way through the courts, Catholic dissent intensified. Legal historian Alan Westin recounts that a group of Catholic writers, teachers, editors and lawyers decided that "more than individual statements would be necessary if the American public were to understand the division of Catholic opinion." They resolved to file a brief in the Supreme Court, "as Catholics, taking the opposite side."

The Archdiocese thereupon summoned the rebels to a meeting where Monsignor John Middleton of the Chancery office assured them that he was deeply concerned, as they were, over such "extremist actions" by lay Catholic groups as picketing the Metropolitan Opera House over its portrayal of the Church in Verdi's opera *Don Carlo*, or threatening a TV station for showing Charlie Chaplin films. (Chaplin was a well-known leftist.) Middleton "went on to suggest that a better result might be achieved for both the Church and cultural freedom if the Committee did not file a brief in the Supreme Court. . . . If the Committee withdrew, Monsignor Middleton suggested, the views of the Committee would be solicited by the Chancery in future censorship issues."

So, the Committee of Catholics for Cultural Action folded its tents—"out of consideration," it explained, "for the larger ambiguities in the situation and out of filial deference" to Cardinal Spellman. The result was that, despite deep divisions on the issue among Christians, the only brief to the Supreme Court representing Christianity came from the State Catholic Committee, in support of banning *The Miracle*.

As for the motion picture industry, it kept silent in the Supreme Court, as it had during the entire controversy. Spellman's biographer John Cooney writes,

> The business, plagued with federal investigators scouring Hollywood for Communists, was running scared. Movie moguls didn't need to be singled out by anti-Communist Catholics. They bent over backward to appease modern inquisitors such as Spellman and the Legion of Decency.

Cooney might have added that Hollywood had long ago made its peace with the Catholic hierarchy, and in fact used it to standardize film content and appease local censorship boards. Now, with Church and state combining to suppress a work that would plainly not have passed muster under the Production Code, the industry was stuck in a dilemma of its own creation.

Building a Case Against Censorship

Ephraim London faced several hurdles in the *Miracle* case, not least of which was the 1915 Supreme Court decision in *Mutual Film*, announcing that movies are not protected by the First Amendment. In a 1948 antitrust decision, Justice William O. Douglas had taken note of this anomaly, writing for the Court that "moving pictures, like newspapers and radio, are included in the press whose freedom is guaranteed by the First Amendment." But the New York Court of Appeals in its *Miracle* decision had dismissed this comment as mere *dicta*, so it was up to London to persuade the justices to overrule the *Mutual Film* case.

At oral argument in *Burstyn v. Wilson* on April 24, 1952, Chief Justice Fred Vinson queried the New York Solicitor General on this question, and got him to admit that, yes, movies do have First Amendment protection. But this didn't mean that all licensing requirements are unconstitutional. Ephraim London, arguing that "a movie cannot ever be censored in advance," got into an argument with Justice Sherman Minton on this point. "Not even for obscenity?" Minton asked. London said: "That's right." It was a position the Supreme Court would reject in its *Burstyn* decison the following month.

The Court's May 1952 decision in *Burstyn v. Wilson* did inter the archaic ruling in *Mutual Film* that cinema is only a business, not a form of expression. It did not follow, however, according to the Court, that all prior-restraint licensing is unconstitutional. Justice Clark's opinion left open the question whether states can impose prior censorship "under a clearly drawn statute designed and applied to prevent the showing of obscene films."

Nine years later, the Court flatly rejected a constitutional challenge to prior-restraint film licensing—over an impassioned dissent by Chief Justice Earl Warren, which enumerated many examples of absurd and bigoted censorship decisions still being perpetrated by state and local licensing boards. But four years after that, the Court finally crippled prior-restraint censorship by invalidating Maryland's licensing scheme because it did not provide for prompt judicial review of determinations that a film was obscene. Stripped of their freewheeling power to ban films without first going to court, the licensing boards finally faded away.

The Demise of Church Control

In writing about the *Miracle* case, Bosley Crowther, then film critic of *The New York Times*, suggested that the Church made a such a fuss over the limited-audience art film precisely because it represented a new breed of foreign movies that were not subject to the Church's control. Even though *Burstyn* as a legal matter involved only official government censorship, it weakened the industry's privately enforced Code by opening the U.S. market to foreign films that looked at life in all its "rawness and reality," and were not submitted in advance to Hollywood's censors.

Critic Gilbert Seldes in *The Nation* magazine made another important point. As Quigley, Breen, and others had perceived, a private industry code, strictly enforced, is more effective than government censorship as a means of imposing religious dogma. It is secret, for one thing, operating at the pre-production stage. The audience never knows what has been trimmed, cut, revised, or never written. For another, it is uniform—not subject to hundreds of different licensing standards. Finally and most important, private censorship can be more sweeping in its demands, because it is not bound by constitutional due process or free-expression rules—in general, these only apply to the government—or by the command of church-state separation.

Hollywood nevertheless did finally get rid of the Production Code in the 1960s. In its place, the MPAA's new head, Jack Valenti, created the vague and subjective rating system that we know today. Movie ratings are decided in secret, and are not without censorial effects. Producers negotiate with the ratings board and cut scenes or dialogue in order to achieve a desired classification. But there is no question that American cinema today is far freer than in the heyday of the Code, when Joe Breen's blue pencil and the Legion of Decency's ever-present boycott threat combined to assure that films adhered to Church doctrine.

THE
HISTORY
OF
ISSUES

CHAPTER 3

Wartime Censorship

Chapter Preface

When the United States began a war against terrorism after the attacks of September 11, 2001, the American tradition of freedom of expression came under intense scrutiny Some argued that the free dissemination of opinions and information compromised national security, while others insisted that upholding people's free speech is an essential American right. This heightened debate over censorship during this time of conflict is not new; a reevaluation of First Amendment boundaries has accompanied every war in U.S. history. Wartime censorship is often initiated to prevent the leaking of information that might be useful to an enemy. Military locations, operational objectives, and battlefield tactics are kept top secret until they are of no possible use to enemy forces. During war, censorship may also involve limiting the information or media coverage that can be made available to the public.

From the Civil War years of mid-nineteenth century to the war with Iraq in the twenty-first century, the American government has implemented official censorship when it perceives a "clear and present danger." Abraham Lincoln first used this standard to censor the mail sent by soldiers and to silence anti-Union newspapers. During World War I, the Sedition Act of 1918 criminalized abusive speech about the flag, the Constitution, and the government. A Federal Censorship Board also ordered "subversive" books to be removed from libraries and cracked down on those who opposed the draft. During World War II, the catchphrase "loose lips sink ships" became common as citizens were discouraged from sharing sensitive information. It was considered illegal to encourage insubordination among the military or disloyalty to the government. Similar restrictions were implemented during subsequent conflicts in Korea, Vietnam, Grenada, Afghanistan, Iraq—and other military struggles.

Americans today hold differing opinions about wartime censorship. Some criticize the lack of restraint shown by the news media and accuse the press of exposing American vulnerabilities in national security during times of war. They believe that the publication of military information and political secrets can help terrorists learn how to be more effective. Others challenge the contention that the freedom of the press is dangerous to national security in the fight against terrorism. They assert that a free press increases the safety of American citizens by providing them with essential information about national vulnerabilities and the solutions proposed by various leaders. Journalists, they argue, help to pressure those charged with protecting the nation to be more accountable to the public. In short the ability to regulate the dissemination of information during wartime is a powerful tool but is also controversial in a democratic society that values freedom of speech.

Military Secrets and Press Censorship

C. Robert Zelnick

In this selection C. Robert Zelnick draws on his experience as a former Pentagon correspondent for ABC News to analyze the evolving relationship between the government and the media during times of war throughout American history. Zelnick writes that government policy about press coverage of military operations has changed many times. Before the Civil War, there was little censorship of journalists covering war stories. However, the development of the telegraph in the 1850s increased the speed that breaking news stories could reach the public and officials, causing Civil War generals to deny journalists access to information that might compromise military strategies. World War I and World War II press dispatches were required to pass through committees that often censored military information, Zelnick writes. In contrast, reporters covering the Vietnam War experienced little official censorship. However, restrictions on media access in the war zone increased after the Vietnam War, making it more difficult for reporters to cover operations in Grenada, the Persian Gulf, and Afghanistan. Zelnick currently serves as the chair of the Department of Journalism at Boston University.

O n June 26, 1993, the U.S. Navy launched twenty-three Tomahawk cruise missiles at Iraq's military intelligence headquarters in Al Mansour, an affluent suburb of Baghdad, to retaliate for Saddam Hussein's alleged plot to kill former President George Bush during the latter's visit to Kuwait. That afternoon, the late Secretary of Defense Les Aspin joined President Bill Clinton, National Security Adviser Anthony Lake,

C. Robert Zelnick, *Rights vs. Public Safety After 9/11: America in the Age of Terrorism.* Lanham, MD: Rowman & Littlefield, 2003. Copyright © 2003 by Rowman & Littlefield Publishers, Inc. An earlier version appeared in the University of Mississippi *Journal of National Security Law,* 1997. Reproduced by permission.

and others in the Oval Office. They hoped to get early confirmation that the missiles had struck the intended target. As might have been expected, television sets were tuned to CNN, but this time with an even greater sense of urgency because U.S. reconnaissance satellites were not favorably positioned to monitor the results of the attack.

When the intended time for the strike passed with no news reports of unusual activity, Secretary Aspin called General Colin Powell at the Pentagon command center. "Could the Tomahawks possibly have missed?" asked the worried secretary.

"Not all of them," replied Powell.

In "desperation," presidential assistant David Gergen called Tom Johnson, president of CNN News. Gergen informed Johnson about the launch and asked him to check with his man in Baghdad in case the reporter had slept through the attack.

The inquiry did not come at the most fortuitous moment for Johnson. His reporters had apprised him only a day or two earlier that a military reprisal against Iraq was likely. However, CNN had not been able to get its own satellite uplink closer than Amman, Jordan, and was relying solely on its radio stringer in the Iraqi capital. In addition, Johnson had a policy against providing the government with information not reported on the air. Like countless other Western journalists and news executives operating in nations with no tradition of political freedom, he knew officials in such nations tend to "mirror image" the relationship between the press and the government. They assume the former to be an adjunct of the latter as active intelligence services when operating abroad. While working in such countries, Johnson took extra care not to reinforce such perceptions.

Johnson had just received reports that missiles were striking the outskirts of Baghdad, some hitting the intelligence facility and others missing. With the information about to go on the air, Johnson bent his policy to the extent of apprising the White House what CNN was "reporting." Moments later, a relieved White House watched as CNN confirmed the story.

National Security and the Press

The incident, related to me by Secretary Aspin some months later and confirmed by Johnson, reflects one small part of one small piece of a complex mosaic. The relationship between the national security apparatus, including the military, and the press is at times symbiotic, at times antagonistic. It is sometimes described as an "adversarial relationship," but the description would be accurate only if the media and the military were aligned on opposite sides. This, of course, has never been the case. Rather, each has its own role to play, and while each is ultimately a guardian of national freedom and democratic values, their separate missions sometimes put them at cross-purposes.

But we are not talking about a zero-sum game. The press seeks to acquire and disseminate as much relevant information as possible. The military regards information as one among many variables to use and control. Too often the issue is described simplistically as a conflict between First Amendment rights and national security. Both history and experience teach the error of this formulation. While it is certainly possible for a careless dispatch to jeopardize legitimate national security interests, military operations, and the lives of service personnel, the documented instances of such reporting are exceedingly few. In dozens of wars and military operations over the past hundred years, representatives of the press have been privy to highly classified operational details or learned or observed things that could compromise legitimate security needs. In nearly all instances, they acted with restraint and responsibility.

Points of Conflict

Documented incidents of reporting that actually harmed the U.S. military or security interests are nonexistent, although there are a handful of instances where irresponsible press conduct could have produced serious harm. During World War II in the Pacific, for example, the *Chicago Tribune* published a report from one of its Pacific correspondents, Stanley Johnson, listing the names of the Japanese warships involved in the Battle of Midway. This information could only have come from coded Japanese communications intercepted and "cracked" by U.S. intelligence. Fortunately, the Japanese failed to read the *Chicago Tribune* and did not alter their encryption regime.

In Korea, General MacArthur's brilliant landing at Inchon was reported before the troops actually hit shore, but again, no damage.

During the Vietnam War, the press had virtually unfettered access to any part of the country, and there was no censorship. Still the media behaved responsibly. When interviewed by the late Peter Braestrup for his definitive study of media-military relations, *Battle Lines*, Barry Zorthian, former spokesman for the U.S. military in Vietnam, stated, "Our leverage was the lifting of credentials, and that was done in only four or five cases, and at least two or three of these were unintentional errors on the part of the correspondent."

Inconsistent Policies

Past efforts to control press coverage of military operations and related matters is a history of inconsistency often rooted more in the whims of individual commanders than logic. Prior to the Civil War, the press faced few, if any, restrictions on its coverage of military operations. The relatively few journalists covering combat and the primitive transportation and communications technologies were decisive checks on the potential to compromise operational details. The development of the telegraph during the 1850s changed that. During the Civil War, Union Generals Ambrose Burnside and William T. Sherman either denied access completely to journalists or kept them at a considerable distance from the story. Meanwhile, an ad hoc censorship regime proved powerful enough to shut down the *Chicago Times* for its incessant attacks on President Lincoln.

When the United States entered World War I in April 1917, the State, Navy, and War Departments established the Committee on Public Information to provide information and enforce censorship regulations. Voluntarily accepted by the press, the regulations forbade publication of such information as "troop movements within the United States, ship sailings, and the identification of units dispatched overseas." In addition, Congress passed the Espionage Act of 1917, which prohibited publication of information useful to the enemy or any interference with military operations or war production, and the Sedition Act of 1918, which banned critical remarks about the conduct of operations, the U.S. government, or its military forces, including the flag. In each case, penalties could include imprisonment for up to twenty years and fines up to $10,000. Press dispatches from the war zone were initially subjected to censorship by a single former *New York Herald* reporter and Associated Press correspondent, Frederick Palmer, and later by a committee of former journalists commissioned as reserve Army officers. The process functioned chaotically. The committee ultimately revoked the credentials of five of the sixty journalists assigned to cover the war. None of this prevented a United Press International reporter from prematurely breaking a story that the armistice had been signed, a breach of security that resulted in the committee temporarily blocking communication between the reporter and his New York headquarters.

Immediately after Pearl Harbor, Congress enacted the War Powers Act, which included the creation of an Office of Censorship. The new office quickly promulgated guidelines, later codified into the Code of Wartime Practices, which took effect January 15, 1942. This code implemented essentially the same types of security restrictions applied during World War I but without the Espionage and Sedition Acts. Throughout the war, the code governed journalists in most combat zones, including the European and North African theaters. In the Pacific, General Douglas MacArthur and the Navy's chief of operations, Admiral Ernest J. King, imposed additional restraints on the press. In fact, years later, the Gannett Foundation's "Media at War" report explained that

> MacArthur required each correspondent's copy to go through a multiple censorship review before being released, and pressured journalists to produce stories that burnished the image of the troops and their supreme commander. The Navy, for its part, delayed the release of news, frequently waiting until a story of combat success could be paired with one describing a setback.

Turning Point: Vietnam

Vietnam marked a turning point in relations between the military and the press. It was the first military conflict subject to daily television coverage. Only a few hardy reporters initially covered the conflict, but by 1968, more than 2,000 accredited reporters were involved. During the conflict, the press routinely applied the term "credibility gap" to military claims of progress. Many in the military blamed the press for loss of public support for the conflict and the resultant political restrictions on its conduct.

Throughout Vietnam, accredited journalists came and went as they pleased. They "hitchhiked" on military transports and helicopters when available and made their own arrangements where necessary. There was virtually no censorship. Instead, the Military Assistance Command, Vietnam (MACV), headquarters for the U.S. effort, asked journalists to refrain from reporting items such as planned offensives, troop movements, and the participation of allied forces in particular operations.

In a technical sense, the rules worked well. Of the thousands of correspondents covering the war, only a handful committed military guideline violations severe enough to result in the revocation of credentials, and only two violations seriously jeopardized operations or safety.

The problem in Vietnam was the deteriorating political relationship between the press and the military. This was partly a reflection and partly a cause of the mounting opposition to the war in the United States. For members of the press, the daily briefings at the Joint U.S. Public Affairs Office (JUSPAO), the office established by MACV to dispense information on the overall effort and supervise coverage by in-country members of the American and foreign media, became known as the "Five O'Clock Follies." This was because briefers often exaggerated political progress and manufactured military victories and enemy casualties. Facetiously, Western newsmen often said, "If it's Vietnamese and it's dead, JUSPAO calls it a Vietcong." As the war continued, reports on the "tactical evacuation" of Vietnamese civilians from their villages; the widespread use of napalm, "Agent Orange," and other defoliants or herbicides; the occasional allied atrocity; the ability of the enemy to mount major operations such as the 1968 Tet offensive; and the horrendous U.S. casualties undoubtedly had a profound impact on public opinion in the United States.

Grenada

The Grenada operation began with a lie and deteriorated from there. In October 1983, Ronald Reagan was president. Platoon leaders and company commanders of Vietnam were now the bird colonels. The media's standing had fallen precipitately. For example, a survey found that in 1966, 29 percent of respondents had "a great deal of confidence" in people running the media. That figure fell to 19 percent in 1983, the year of the Grenada invasion (and to 11 percent in 1995). The military took advantage of the fortuitous political circumstances, virtually barring press coverage of the operation, which, contrary to the Pentagon's first accounts, was characterized by spotty intelligence, logistical foul-ups, and bungled execution. In fact, as Peter Braestrup recalls, CBS White House correspondent Bill Plante learned of the operation from a source the day before the invasion. He sought confirmation from White House Press Secretary Larry Speakes, who vetted the information with Bob Sims, the National Security Council press officer, and Admiral John Poindexter, the president's national security adviser. From Poindexter, the word came: "Plante—no invasion of Grenada. Preposterous. Knock it down hard."

Compare that lie with the attitude of Brigadier General Robert A. McClure, the assistant chief of staff at the Supreme Headquarters Allied European Force. Asked whether the Allies should mislead the press regarding the date and location of the Normandy invasion, Braestrup quotes from McClure's note to Sir Cyril Radcliffe of the British Ministry of Information: "Men who profess to present the news honestly should not be subjected to official suasion to present it dishonestly, however laudable the purpose. We cannot remove the foundations of a house and expect it to remain standing." The Allies found other ways to disinform the Germans.

It is possible to see World War II coverage in too rosy a light. After all, the press was usually uniformed, censorship was strict, and reporters were subject to military courts-martial for disobedience. But the access was near total, from amphibious landings to paratroop drops behind enemy lines. Denials of access, beginning with Grenada, had no reasonable military basis. As Major General Winant Sidle, U.S. Army (ret.), who headed a committee that developed procedures governing press activities for military conflicts after Grenada, candidly acknowledged, "Although never admitted, the military's distrust of the media at the time of the Grenada operation in 1983 had to be part of the reason the media were not permitted on Grenada for the first two days, and only a pool was allowed on the third day."

In response, Joint Chiefs of Staff Chairman General John W. Vessey appointed the Sidle Commission, formally known as the Chairman of the Joint Chiefs of Staff Media Military Relations Panel. The commission reviewed the Grenada experience and recommended a more appropriate way for dealing with future operations. Comments from the press were solicited. In his letter to General Sidle dated January 3, 1984, Roone Arledge, president of ABC News, noted,

> On the day our troops landed on Grenada, I wrote to Secretary of Defense Weinberger, saying the practice of journalists accompanying American troops into action was as old as our republic. Now, for the first time in our history, the press was unreasonably excluded from going with American troops into action. In my opinion, no convincing or compelling reason has yet been cited for this unprecedented departure from our tradition of independent press reporting.

On August 23, 1984, General Sidles panel unanimously concluded that "it is essential that the U.S. news media cover U.S. military operations to the maximum degree possible consistent with mission security and the safety of U.S. forces." The panel emphasized that the preferred method of coverage is open access for all journalists assigned to cover the story. The panel also recognized that the pool is necessary to handle atypical situations, as when operations are in remote or otherwise inaccessible areas.

The panel concluded that an adversarial relationship between the press and the military "is healthy" but that "mutual antagonism and distrust are not in the best interests of the media, the military, or the American people." Michael Burch, assistant secretary of defense for public affairs, responded to the Sidle recommendations by saying, "We agree with them all." Secretary of Defense Caspar Weinberger and General Vessey formed a "public affairs cell" in the office of the chairman of the Joint Chiefs of Staff to put the recommendations into practice. . . .

The Persian Gulf War

Coverage of the Persian Gulf War involved efforts by at least 1,400 reporters trying to gain access to military personnel in the field. Some journalists were stationed in Baghdad, while others—the regular core of Pentagon, State Department, White House, and Washington journalists—remained in Washington and hoped to gain information or insight from there. Before the start of Operation Desert Storm, Louis A. "Pete" Williams, the Department of Defense's assistant secretary for public affairs, issued guidelines for coverage with restrictions that fell into familiar and acceptable categories. The press could not provide coverage regarding specific numbers of troops, aircraft, or weapons systems; details of future plans, operations, or strikes; information on the specific location of military forces or security arrangements in effect; rules of engagement; intelligence collection activities; troop movements; identification of aircraft origin; effectiveness or ineffectiveness of enemy camouflage, cover, deception, or targeting; specific information on downed aircraft or damaged ships while search-and-rescue missions were planned or under way; and information on operational or support vulnerabilities of U.S. and allied forces.

By all accounts, including the Pentagon's, the U.S. military handled the press poorly. Then-Secretary of Defense Dick Cheney set the tone initially when he refused to let reporters accompany the first U.S. troops to the region on August 8, 1990, because Saudi Arabia declined to permit it. Several months after the war, a committee of seventeen senior news executives from the networks, leading wire services, newspapers, and weeklies circulated a fourteen-page report on the military's handling of the press titled "Independent Reporting: Prevention Of."

Still, the media tried to get as much of the story as possible. Those who could assigned reporters to Baghdad. Many print reporters braved military resistance and operated unilaterally, as did such network correspondents as Forrest Sawyer of ABC News, who eventually linked up with advancing Egyptian units, and Bob McKeown of CBS, who became the first television correspondent to report live from liberated Kuwait City. Both Sawyer's and McKeown's work provided a hint of the next stage in the difficult media-military relationship as the media's ability to report in real time came increasingly in conflict with the legitimate military need to avoid presenting the other side with instant battlefield intelligence. Throughout the Persian Gulf War, however, most reporters on the scene were reduced to sitting through press briefings in Riyadh asking questions that reflected the silliness and hostility of the situation.

Afghanistan

It is interesting to compare the highly restricted coverage of Operation Desert Shield and Operation Desert Storm with the work of the press in reporting on the Shiite and Kurdish rebellions after the war. With no pools, no escorts, no "restricted" areas, and no "Saudi sensibilities" to worry about, journalists, in the full exercise of their First Amendment rights, documented the horrors being perpetrated by Saddam Hussein and countenanced by the [George] Bush administration. The result was a prompt and substantial change in U.S. policy, which the president and his advisers would later attribute not to the media but to the desire to keep Iraq's Kurds from flooding neighboring Turkey. For more than a year following the cessation of hostilities in the Persian Gulf, Pentagon officials and a committee consisting mainly of the same individuals who had published the "Independent Reporting" document reviewed the experience. They sought to reach an accord on new and more satisfactory procedures to govern future conflicts. Eventually, they agreed on nine principles—including the stipulations that "journalists will have access to all major military units" and that "military public affairs officers should act as liaisons but should not interfere with the reporting process"—and "agreed to disagree" over the question of "prior security review," or censorship.

Then came [the war in] Afghanistan, and, at least in its early days, most of the good intentions were relegated to their traditional mission, paving the road to hell. Reporters had difficulty gaining access to the carriers supporting the operation or the pilots returning from strike missions. Bases in nearby Uzbekistan and Tajikistan were off limits because of local sensibilities. Accompanying special forces was out of the question. Reporters at one base camp were herded into a warehouse to keep them away from troops returning from a "friendly fire" accident. On one occasion, a *Washington Post* reporter was stopped at gunpoint from inspecting collateral damage from bombs dropped by an unmanned U.S. drone. As the war continued and U.S. success mounted, access became somewhat easier.

A Minimal Threat

While conflicts between First Amendment values and national security needs are a long-running source of legal analysis and intellectual fascination, during the past generation it has become clear that such conflicts are truly aberrational. The press rarely poses any kind of danger to national security. The goal of defense officials, military or civilian, who seek to keep the press on a short leash is, in most instances, to control the editorial slant of what is reported rather than to protect tactical, strategic, or national security from the unauthorized disclosure of sensitive material.

Government Censorship During World War I

Robert Justin Goldstein

The opposition to American participation in World War I was extensive. In reaction to this opposition, federal and local government often administered a policy of repression and censorship to silence dissenting voices. In this selection historian Robert Justin Goldstein documents government crackdowns during World War I on progressive and antiwar activists and organizations, including socialists and anarchists, the International Workers of the World, and the National Labor Party. Legislation such as the Espionage, Sedition, and Alien Acts were imposed in the name of national security to outlaw criticism of the government and imprison those who spoke against the war. The American Protective League was organized by President Woodrow Wilson to empower volunteers from across the country to investigate the loyalty of soldiers and government personnel, Goldstein writes. Freedom of the press was curtailed when the U.S. Post Office Department banned distribution of newspapers that published opposition to government policies. Goldstein is a professor of political science at Oakland University in Rochester, Michigan, and the author of numerous books about civil liberties, including Political Repression in Modern America from 1870 to 1976.

Given the strength of the radical movement in 1917, it is not surprising that opposition to American participation in the war was enormous. There is a tenacious myth that antiwar feelings during World War I were neglible after American entry, but such a position is simply not supported by the facts. Although the Wilson administration eventually succeeded in generating a considerable amount of war hysteria

Robert Justin Goldstein, *Political Repression in Modern America from 1870 to 1976*Champaign: University of Illinois Press, 2001. Copyright © 2001 by the Board of Trustees of the University of Illinois. Reproduced by permission of the author.

through its propaganda agency, the Committee on Public Information (CPI), when the U.S. first entered the war, "throughout the country, and especially in the middle west, influential groups of people were apathetic if not actually hostile to fighting [according to historian Thomas A. Bailey]." Fifty-six congressmen voted against the declaration of war, compared with only one such vote against entry into World War II.

Resistance to WWI

Organizations which identified themselves as against the war, or which were identified as such in the public mind, made strong gains during 1917, despite the opening of a vicious campaign of repression against them on the part of the federal, state and local governments. Thus, the IWW [International Workers of the World or "Wobblies"] recruited over thirty thousand new members between April 1, 1917 and September, 1917. During this five-month period alone, IWW income reached over $275,000, compared to a total income of about $50,000 for the entire year ending August 31, 1916.

While the IWW took no formal stand on the war, there can be no question that the SPA's [Socialist Party of America] enormous gains during 1917 were a direct reflection of its strong anti-war stand. Shortly after American entry into the war, a special convention of the SPA overwhelmingly adopted a position of "unalterable opposition" to American entry and called for a program of "continuous, active and public opposition to the war, through demonstrations, mass petitions and all other means within our power," including opposition to conscription and opposition to raising money to pay for the war. This program was ratified by an SPA membership vote of over twenty-one thousand to less than three thousand.

In the two months following adoption of this position, which President Wilson referred to in his private correspondence as "almost treasonable", SPA membership jumped more than twelve thousand. In the fall, 1917, municipal elections, the party's vote reached what even an extremely hostile historian [Daniel Bell] has conceded were "new spectacular heights." A survey of the party's vote in fourteen cities showed the SPA polled an average of 21.6 percent of the vote, a total which if projected nationally would have meant four million votes, compared with the previous high of less than one million votes in a presidential election. In city after city the party registered remarkable gains, frequently increasing its vote fivefold compared with the last previous election in the various cities. In New York City, the SPA mayoral candidate received 21.7 percent, while the party elected aldermanic candidates for the first time and elected ten state assemblymen, compared to a previous high of two. In Chicago, the SPA got nearly 34 percent of the vote; in Buffalo 25 percent; in Dayton 44 percent; in Toledo 35 percent. Altogether the party received from 20 percent to 50 percent of the vote in a dozen of the largest cities in Ohio, in ten towns and cities in Pennsylvania, in six cities in Indiana, and in four in New York. SPA support was heaviest in working class districts, including both immigrant areas and areas dominated by native workers.

Despite repeated attacks upon its patriotism the NPL [National Labor Party] also continued to gain support during 1917. While the NPL formally backed the war effort, it did not hesitate to criticize many local and federal governmental policies. For example, the League called for the "conscription of wealth" to finance the war, and urged the federal government to nationalize basic elements of the economy. Despite this position and severe repression, the NPL continued to make gains in Minnesota and elsewhere.

The People's Council of America for Peace and Democracy, an umbrella anti-war organization, organized in May, 1917, also gained a large public following. Thousands of persons attended rallies called by the Council across the country, even in small towns like Moline and Rock Island, Illinois. In August, 1917, Ralph Easley of the [National Civic Federation

(NCF)] wrote that "how to neutralize the campaign being waged through the country in the interest of 'an early peace' under the guise of the so-called People's Council" was the question of the day; he lamented that "mass meetings are held nightly and are enthusiastically attended in the big industrial centers from Maine to California."

Opposition to the war was by no means confined to organized groups of radicals, however. A total of over three hundred thirty thousand draft evaders or delinquents were reported during the war. The draft was immensely unpopular everywhere; as many as 60 percent of those registering requested exemptions.

Charles S. Barrett, president of the Farmers Educational and Cooperative Union, told the pro-war League for National Unity in September, 1917, that anti-war sentiment was prevalent among southern farmers. In November, George Creel, chairman of the CPI, reported that, "You will find in Georgia and parts of South Carolina, you will find in Arkansas; you will find in many parts of the West, an indifference that is turned into a very active irritation that borders on disloyalty. . . . We must take on the whole country."

Federal Repression of the Anti-War Movement

Given the tremendous amount of opposition to American participation in the war, the severe governmental repression which developed did not constitute an irrational response. Anti-war sentiment did not pose a threat of revolution or violence, but it did pose a threat of spreading disaffection which could paralyze the war effort. Thus the "progressive" Wilson administration quickly embarked upon a program of repression that matched or exceeded wartime repression even in clearly totalitarian countries such as Germany and Russia, and which clearly exceeded the degree of repression experienced by America's Anglo-Saxon partner, Great Britain. Thus in many cases during World War I American citizens were sent to jail for up to twenty years for mere verbal opposition to the war, offenses "which at the most would have drawn from any English court a sentence of a few months in jail or a medium-sized fine [writes historian Robert E. Cushman]."

The general climate of repression which quickly enveloped the country was set up by the very highest levels of the federal government. Addressing the Congress on April 2, 1917 to ask for a declaration of war, Wilson warned that Germany had "filled our unsuspecting communities and even our offices of government with spies and set criminal intrigues everywhere afoot against our national unity of counsel, our peace within and without, our industries and our commerce." He warned, "If there should be disloyalty it will be dealt with a firm hand of stern repression." In June, 1917, Wilson warned that "the masters of Germany" were using "liberals, . . . socialists, the leaders of labor" to "carry out their designs" and that "it is only friends and partisans of the German government whom we have already identified who utter these thinly disguised disloyalties. . . . Woe be to the man or group of men that seeks to stand in our way in this day of high resolution." Attorney General Thomas Gregory, referring to war opponents in November, 1917, stated, "May God have mercy on them, for they need expect none from an outraged people and an avenging government."

The Espionage and Sedition Acts

The two major legislative weapons of repression wielded by the federal government were the Espionage Act of June 15, 1917 and the Sedition Act of May 16, 1918. The Espionage Act, which consisted of an amalgamation of various bills prepared in the Attorney General's office, provided for punishment of up to twenty years in jail and a $10,000 fine for those who during wartime "wilfully" made false statements with "intent to interfere with the operation or success of the military or naval forces or to promote the success of its enemies" or who "wilfully" caused or attempted to cause "insubordination, disloyalty, mutiny or refusal of duty" in the armed forces or "wilfully" obstructed armed forces recruitment or enlistment. Another provision of the bill provided that the Post Office could exclude from the mails any matter violating provisions of the act or "advocating or urging treason, insurrection or re-sistance to any law of the U.S." Despite strenuous efforts by President Wilson, Congress defeated another proposed section of the act which would have provided authority to directly censor the press.

The Sedition Act, also passed with the support of the Wil-son administration, outlawed virtually all criticism of the war or the government. Among the types of activities outlawed by it were making statements or performing acts favoring the cause of any country at war with the U.S. or opposing the cause of the U.S. therein; making false statements that would obstruct the sale of war bonds, incite disloyalty or obstruct enlistment; and uttering, printing or publishing any "disloyal, profane, scurrilous or abusive language about the form of government of the U.S. or the constitution of the U.S., or the military or naval forces of the U.S. or the flag of the U.S. or the uniform of the army or navy" or any language intended to bring these institutions into "contempt, scorn, contumely or disrepute."

Additional Censorship Laws

The federal government also had a whole arsenal of other weapons to silence dissenters. On April 6, 1917, Wilson issued a proclamation establishing regulations for the conduct and control of enemy aliens, under the Alien Enemies Act of 1798, a law passed during the Alien and Sedition era. This procla-mation made all enemy aliens subject to summary arrest. At the same time, the Attorney General approved publication of a statement assuring German aliens that they had nothing to fear so long as they were not implicated in plots against American interests and they agreed to obey the law and "keep your mouth shut." As hysteria about potential German spies escalated, Wilson issued new orders in the fall of 1917 requiring all German aliens fourteen years of age and older to register with the government, and barred all such persons from a variety of places deemed to be of military importance, expelled them from Washington, D.C., required them to get permission to travel within the U.S. or to change their place of residence, and barred access to all ships and boats except public ferries. Altogether these regulations affected about six hundred thousand German-Americans, and led to the arrest of sixty-three hundred enemy aliens and the internment in concentration camps of twenty-three hundred who were alleged to be dangerous to the national security. Perhaps the most famous internee under this program was Dr. Carl Muck, conductor of the Boston Symphony Orchestra, whose main crimes appear to have been declining for a time to play the national anthem at the beginning of concerts and associating with German diplomats in the U.S. He was arrested and interned in March, 1918, just in time to prevent him from conducting Bach's *Passion According to Saint Matthew.*

Under the February, 1917, law barring threats against the President, sixty cases were brought by June, 1918. Many of these cases were clearly ludicrous. For example, one man was sent to jail for saying, "I wish Wilson was in hell, and if I had the power, I would put him there." The judge in this case reasoned that Wilson "could not be in the state called hell until life was terminated," and thus this statement constituted a threat against the President's life.

On April 7, 1917, Wilson instituted a program for the summary removal of any employee of the federal government deemed "inimical to the public welfare by reason of his conduct, sympathies or utterances, or because of other reasons growing out of the war." Further, the Civil Service Commission (CSC) was authorized to refuse all applications for employment if there was a "reasonable belief" that such employment would be "inimical to the public interest owing to . . . lack of loyalty." While no dismissal figures are available, the *New York Times* reported in July, 1917 that firings under this provision had been "frequent." Thus, one postal clerk was reportedly fired for making statements such as, "To Hell with the Allies." The CSC barred almost nine hundred persons from taking entrance examinations on grounds of questionable loyalty from 1917 to 1921.

Under the Trading with the Enemy Act of October 6, 1917, foreign language newspapers were required to submit to the Post Office for approval, before mailing, translations of all material concerning the government and the war; newspapers which satisfied the President as to their loyalty could be exempted, however. As a result of the financial and editorial problems posed by such delays, by mid-1918, "practically every one of the German newspapers . . . was forced to either adopt a pro-government editorial policy or to maintain a judicious silence on war questions." Scores of German-language newspapers ceased operations altogether as a result of the law. The combined effects of the Trading with the Enemy Act and the general hostility in the country to things German-American reduced the German-American press by 47 percent by the end of 1919; the number of German-language dailies dropped to twenty-six, less than half the prewar figure, and their circulation dropped by two-thirds to about two hundred fifty thousand. In states with a small German ethnic population, the destruction of the German language press was usually total.

On October 16, 1918, Congress completed the legislative arsenal of repression by passing an immigration law which extended the concept of guilt by association, first introduced for the purpose of excluding and deporting individual anarchists and advocates of violence to cover all persons who were *mem-*

bers of organizations which advocated unlawful destruction of property, or the forceful or violent overthrow of the government—a provision aimed squarely at the IWW. Under this law, and the provisions of the immigration law of February, 1917, a total of 687 persons were arrested for deportation by the end of the war. Of these, about 60 had been deported by November 1, 1918, another 88 were under deportation orders, and 162 had had their orders cancelled. While aliens were the major target of action under the immigration laws, in some cases steps were taken to denaturalize naturalized citizens, also. For example, a German immigrant who had been naturalized in 1882 had his citizenship cancelled in 1917 after he refused to contribute to the Red Cross and the Young Men's Christian Association because he refused to do anything to harm his native land. The revocation was based on the contention that he had taken his oath of renunciation in 1882 with a mental reservation.

The strength and scope of various "internal security" agencies was greatly increased during the war. As noted earlier, beginning in March, 1917, the War Department authorized local army officers to "sternly repress acts committed with seditious intent" and to protect "public utilities" essential to the war, criteria which were vague enough to soon cover the smashing of IWW strikes. Military intelligence forces expanded from two officers in early 1917 to thirteen hundred officers and civilian employees by the end of the war, and similar increases occurred in the security agencies of the Justice, Post Office and Treasury Departments. Military intelligence agents participated in a wide range of dubious activities, which involved a wholesale system of spying on civilians that would be unmatched in scope until the late 1960's. Military intelligence activities included surveillance of the IWW, the SPA, the pacifist Fellowship of Reconciliation and the National Civil Liberties Bureau, forerunner of the American Civil Liberties Union. In some cases, military intelligence infiltrated the ranks of groups under surveillance and participated in raids and arrests of radical organizations. Military intelligence investigated one southern governor for his alleged "radical" leanings, and broke one strike in Butte, Montana by an illegal raid and jailing without charges of over seventy IWW members. Later, it turned out that the Butte strike had apparently been provoked by undercover military intelligence officers working with Anaconda copper company detectives. One military intelligence officer recommended that a federal judge be replaced by a man who would be a "500 percent American."

The American Protective League

Certainly the most novel security force organized by the Wilson administration during the war was the American Protective League (APL), a privately-funded volunteer organization which operated with the endorsement of the Justice Department. The official purpose of the APL, which numbered three hundred fifty thousand persons by the end of the war, was to help the government with such matters as food rationing and putting the conscription machinery into operation, along with specific intelligence operations such as investigating the loyalty of soldiers and governmental personnel and (when for the first time in American history passports were introduced in 1917) investigating the loyalty of Americans who wished to leave the country for any reason. However, the organization quickly became a largely out-of-control quasi-governmental, quasi-vigilante agency which established a massive spy network across the land. The relationship between the APL and the Justice Department and whether or not APL members had the right to make arrests was deliberately left vague, allowing APL operatives to claim they were an arm of the government and had the right to make arrests. Along with illegal arrests and detentions, APL agents instigated attacks on radicals and disrupted meetings of unions and socialists. Some APL members infiltrated radical organizations, and some burglarized, wiretapped, bugged and opened the mail of such groups. Beginning in January, 1918, APL operatives began to collect information "on all rumors current in their communities which they considered to be harmful to the interests of the United States in the prosecution of the war;" as a result by the autumn of that year "there were few actions or attitudes of American people which were not duly noted by the APL and referred either to the Justice Department or to the War Department." The Justice Department did not impose even minimal controls on APL activity until late 1918.

The APL tended to be composed of the "upper social, economic and political crust of each community" and this was frequently reflected in both its legal and illegal activities. Thus, the head of the APL urged his chief lieutenants to obtain financial support from leading businessmen "who usually are the ones benefited in a property sense by the protection afforded by our organization." Some APL operatives acted as labor spies for employers, while others pressured colleges to fire radical professors and librarians to take suspect material off the shelves. John Roche's characterization of the APL as a "government-sponsored lynch-mob which proudly took the law into its own hands in summary and brutal fashion" was accurate all too often.

Slacker Raids

APL members were active, along with Justice Department agents, local police and federal troops in so-called "slacker raids" which took part in many American cities between April and September, 1918. During these raids, which were designed to detect persons who had failed to register for the draft, thousands of wholly innocent people were seized and often detained in jail cells overnight if they could not produce draft cards. Men were seized from street corners, railroad stations, hotels, theatres, streetcars, saloons, pool rooms and dance, halls. Thus, in Chicago during three days of raids in July,

1918, an estimated one hundred fifty thousand men were interrogated and sixteen thousand were arrested on suspicion of being slackers, of whom twelve hundred (about 8 percent of those arrested) were found to be evaders and two hundred sixty-five (about 2 percent of those arrested) were found to be deserters. The most notorious slacker raids occurred in New York City in September, 1918. Over ten thousand persons (according to some reports, twenty thousand to forty thousand persons) were arrested during the raids; in one case the exists to a theatre were blocked and all playgoers who could not produce draft cards were arrested. Troops had to be called in to disperse crowds of anxious relatives gathered before an armory where some of the arrested men were held. Less than 1 percent of those arrested turned out to be draft dodgers. The New York raids caused an immense storm of criticism in the Senate. Sen. Albert Fall, a conservative who later went to jail during the Teapot Dome scandals, commented about the slacker raids, "Never in the history of any civilized country under the heavens, except in the history of Russia, could such acts have been committed." Attorney General Gregory later said his orders against the use of APL men and military men making actual arrests had been ignored, but otherwise defended the raids; at the same time, for the first time the Justice Department clearly told APL members that they did not have arrest powers. APL slacker raids continued, using federal or local police to make the actual arrests. By the end of the war APL raids had netted about forty thousand "slackers," a figure suggesting that over four hundred thousand men were arrested in the course of the raids, since most of those arrested were later released.

Beyond the Law

Unauthorized and illegal activities by military intelligence and the APL were not unusual during the war, but even Justice Department agents, presumably under the direct control of

Gregory, sometimes acted on their own. Thus, in September, 1918 Justice Department agents acting without Gregory's approval sacked the offices of the NCLB.

Gregory's inability to control his subordinates was a common experience among high-ranking federal officials during the war. Secretary of Labor William B. Wilson repeatedly instructed officials of the Bureau of Immigration that aliens could not be arrested for deportation solely for IWW membership, but immigration officials, particularly in the Seattle area, continually violated these instructions. Secretary of War Newton D. Baker took an extremely generous and lenient view on the treatment of conscientious objectors, but lower ranking military commanders repeatedly ignored his instructions and treated objectors with extreme brutality. CO's were sometimes severely beaten, placed in solitary confinement, handcuffed for hours to cell bars, fed only bread and water, pricked with bayonets and/or immersed head first in the filth of camp latrines. Pressure on the conscientious objectors at military camps was so scvcrc that although 20,873 men arrived at camps with draft board certificates supporting their claims, eventually only 3,989 refused to accept any kind of military duty. Senator George W. Norris commented that if the reports he had received about treatment of the CO's were "anywhere near the truth ... we are more barbarous in the treatment of these unfortunate men, than were the men of the Dark Ages in the treatment of their prisoners." Eventually, 540 objectors were court-martialled, while in England such persons received sentences which did not exceed two years. In the U.S. 17 were sentenced to death, 142 to life in prison, and 345 to jail terms averaging sixteen and one-half years. With the quick termination of the war, none of the death sentences or lengthy prison terms were carried out.

Federal Weapons of Censorship

While the APL, military intelligence, deportation arrests and summary internment of enemy aliens were widely used to suppress dissent, the Espionage and Sedition Acts and the use of federal troops were probably the most important federal weapons of repression. The application of the Espionage and Sedition Acts was a combination of random terror, and carefully directed prosecutions designed to destroy the IWW and the SPA. The random terror resulted from the fact that the Justice Department made no serious attempt until very late in the war to veto the attempts of overzealous local U.S. district attorneys to prosecute in questionable cases. Thus, prosecutions were highly related to the character of federal attorneys and varied greatly from area to area, with prosecutions in thirteen of the eighty-seven federal districts accounting for almost half of the total number of prosecutions. In October 1918, President Wilson expressed concern to Attorney General Gregory that the failure to control local district attorneys had created the "danger of playing into the hands of some violently and maliciously partisan Republicans." After the November, 1918, Congressional elections, in which Democrats lost heavily, GPI Director Greel wrote to Wilson that the election had turned out as it did because:

> All the radical or liberal friends of your anti-imperialist war policy were either silenced or intimidated. The Department of Justice and the Post Office were allowed to silence and intimidate them. There was no voice to argue for your sort of peace.

Altogether, over twenty-one hundred were indicted under the Espionage and Sedition laws, invariably for statements of opposition to the war rather than for any overt acts, and over one thousand persons were convicted. Over one hundred persons were sentenced to jail terms of ten years or more. Not a single person was ever convicted for actual spy activities.

Many espionage and sedition indictments were brought for making statements of a clearly innocuous nature, and in some cases prosecutions were brought as a result of statements made in private conversations. Men were prosecuted for making statements such as the following: "We must make the world safe for democracy, even if we have to bean the goddess of liberty to do it;" "Men conscripted to Europe are virtually condemned to death and everyone knows it;" "I am for the people and the government is for the profiteers." One man was sentenced to twenty years in prison for stating in a private conversation that atrocity stories were lies, that the war was "a rich man's war and the U.S. is simply fighting for money" and that he hoped the "government goes to hell so it will be of no value." Another man got twenty years for circulating a pamphlet urging the re-election of a Congressman who had voted against conscription. In Louisiana, a state senator was indicted for writing that profiteers would take advantage of the war to establish financial slavery. A northerner with a German name who exclaimed, "Damn such a country as this," when he found Florida's weather unexpectedly chilly was arrested for violating the Espionage Act, as was a Mennonite farmer whose religious principles would not permit him to support the war, on the grounds that he had desecrated the flag after a mob seized him and trampled on a flag which had been thrust into his hand and had fallen to the ground.

The producer of a movie called "The Spirit of '76" was given ten years in jail after it was alleged that by showing British atrocities during the American Revolution he tended to raise questions about the good faith of America's war-time ally. Probably the single most incredible case was that of Walter Matthey of Iowa, who was sentenced to a year in jail, for, according to Attorney General Gregory, "attending a meeting, listening to an address in which disloyal utterances were made, applauding some of the statements made by the speaker claimed to be disloyal, their exact nature not being known and contributing 25¢."

Suppression of the Press

Many of the actions of the Post Office Department in denying the use of the mails to newspapers and other publications also smacked of random terrorism. The first newspaper Attorney General Albert Burleson removed from the mails (even before Wilson signed the Espionage Act) was the Halletsville, Texas, *Rebel*, which, coincidentally, had exposed the eviction of tenant farmers and their replacement by unpaid tenant labor in land Burleson owned. Other publications that were barred including Lenin's *Soviets at Work*; an issue of *The Public*, for urging that more of the wartime budget be raised by taxation and less by loan; the *Freeman's Journal and Catholic Register*, for reprinting Jefferson's opinion that Ireland should be free; the *Irish World*, for stating that Palestine would be retained by Great Britain on the same footing as Egypt, and that the trend of French life and ideals for a century had been toward materialism; and NCLB pamphlets deploring mob violence and explaining the beliefs of conscientous objectors. Altogether seventy-five papers were interfered with in one way or another.

If much of the government's repressive activity seemed to be random terrorism, much of it was not. It was certainly not just happenstance that the two major anarchist publications, *Mother Earth*, and *Blast*, were quickly banned from the mails and that anarchist leaders Goldman and Berkman were jailed for conspiracy to violate the conspiracy act; that the editors of the *Messenger*, one of the few black publications that refused to back the war all-out were jailed and the paper banned from the mails; that the *Jeffersonian*, a paper published by the former Georgia populist leader Tom Watson was banned from the mails after receiving over $100,000 in contributions to challenge the constitutionality of the conscription act; and that in raids and arrests throughout the country the entire executive committee of the Jehovah's Witnesses was convicted for their published opposition to the killing of any human being.

Even the seemingly random prosecutions had a pattern behind them however; persons or publications "who had assured economic and social status, did not question the basis of our economic system, accepted the war as a holy crusade and expressed their views in somewhat temperate language" were allowed to criticize the government; those who suffered were "those whose views on the war were derived from some objectionable economic or social doctrines ... regardless of their attitude towards Germany" along with obscure individuals who used "indiscreet or impolite, sometimes vulgar language to express their views." Certainly the strong attacks made by many congressmen and leading newspapers about arms and ammunition shortages and inadequate housing in the army was bound to depress morale in the armed forces more than private statements made in opposition to the war, but somehow prominent newspapers and members of the two major parties never suffered at the hands of the Post Office and Justice Departments.

Censorship of the Pentagon Papers During the Vietnam War

John Prados and Margaret Pratt Porter

One of the most famous cases of modern government censorship of the media unfolded in 1971 with the publication of information about the Pentagon Papers in the New York Times. *The Pentagon Papers documented the opinions and choices of U.S. leaders during the early years of the Vietnam War. Disclosing the contents of the report to the public was momentous because its topsecret pages provided evidence of government cover-ups and a policy of dishonesty when reporting to U.S. citizens.*

In this selection writers John Prados and Margaret Pratt Porter explain how Daniel Ellsberg, a government insider, decided to leak the secret Pentagon Papers to the press in order to reveal the truth about the war to the public. After Ellsberg's leak, President Richard Nixon's administration unsuccessfully attempted to prevent the American press from publishing the Pentagon Papers in the name of national security. Prados and Porter argue that government cover-ups like that of the Pentagon Papers are standard practice even today. Prados is a historian who has written numerous books about U.S. involvement in war, including The Blood Road: The Ho Chi Minh Trail and the Vietnam War *and* The President's Secret Wars: CIA and Pentagon Covert Operations from Worm War II Through the Persian Gulf. *Porter is the director of communications and publications for Vietnam Veterans of America and the editor of* VVA Veteran.

On June 13, 1971, the *New York Times* front page carried the first installment of a major series on the Vietnam War, one based upon a massive, top-secret study compiled by

John Prados and Margaret Pratt Porter, *Inside the Pentagon Papers*. Lawrence: University Press of Kansas, 2004. © 2004 by the University Press of Kansas. All rights reserved. Reproduced by permission.

the Pentagon. Under the headline VIETNAM ARCHIVE: PENTAGON STUDY TRACES THREE DECADES OF GROWING U.S. INVOLVEMENT, the *Times* reported on the innermost thoughts of administrations from Harry S Truman's to Lyndon Johnson's during crucial moments of the war from its inception. A related background story noted that the newspaper had acquired a copy of the Pentagon study and promised a series of forthcoming articles that would detail its contents. The *New York Times* story represented the first public revelation of what became known as the "Pentagon Papers" an inside account of U.S. government choices on the Vietnam War that raised eyebrows throughout America, indeed throughout the world.

The Vietnam War Context

It is important today to recapture something of the atmosphere of that moment. The Vietnam War was still in full swing. A new round of intense fighting had begun in the demilitarized zone that separated North and South Vietnam, and just two months before American-backed South Vietnamese forces had pulled out of Laos after failing to break the back of the key North Vietnamese supply route to the South. The president of that day, Richard Nixon, nevertheless insisted the invasion had been a success and had demonstrated the success of his strategy of Vietnamization. Not to be diverted, the Nixon administration had resorted to bombing raids in northern Laos using huge B-52 jet aircraft, all sorts of activities supporting Cambodians who were fighting communist insurgents, and continued military efforts in South Vietnam. The administration was claiming that "understandings" unilaterally declared by the Johnson administration before suspending its bombing campaign against North Vietnam in 1968 gave Nixon's commanders justification for renewed attacks on the North.

Manipulation of information, constant and widespread, remained central to the government's conduct of the Vietnam

War, with the bombing "understandings" only one example. In another egregious case, for years the government had claimed there were no Americans involved in the war in Laos, where the CIA was running a massive coven paramilitary program and the United States steadily furnishing aid to the Laotian armed forces. Richard Nixon actually made a televised public declaration denying U.S. involvement in Laos. American reporters had stumbled into bases for the CIA's secret army of thousands of Hmong tribesmen and had written about them even as the administration continued its denials. Congress had held hearings on the Laotian programs and gotten material onto the record, but when Nixon administration officials released an approved version of the proceedings, data on the U.S. involvement had been concealed by being deemed classified. Similarly misleading maneuvers were undertaken to conceal information on the exact roles Americans played in prisoner interrogations in South Vietnam, the Cambodian invasion, the Laotian incursion, the secret bombing of Cambodia carried out in 1969–1970, and many other instances. American citizens were increasingly forced to question what their government said in its official pronouncements.

Escalating Opposition to the War

The most controversial conflict in U.S. history since the Civil War, the republic had struggled for years to respond to the challenge of Vietnam. By 1968 the consensus had taken hold that the nation had to get out of Vietnam, yet here, three years later, the war ground on. The Nixon administration was gradually pulling its ground forces out of South Vietnam but increasingly relying upon airpower. Driven by their fears for the republic, and by increasingly vocal protests from the public, legislative leaders reacted with horror as the Nixon administration escalated the war, invading Cambodia in 1970 and now Laos. They voted to repeal the original claimed authority for the Vietnam War, the Gulf of Tonkin Resolution, which

Lyndon B. Johnson had gotten in 1964. Then they began offering bills, amendments, riders to legislation, all with the aim of restricting in some fashion Nixon's freedom of action in Southeast Asia. Even after Laos, however, Richard Nixon insisted he would continue the war to free American prisoners and would keep U.S. advisers in Vietnam for as long as they were needed by the U.S.-supported Saigon government.

The Laotian invasion had sparked massive demonstrations on both the East and West Coasts, including a huge march on Washington, a strong protest by Vietnam veterans who threw their medals back at the Capitol, and an effort at civil disobedience by protesters intent on preventing the Nixon administration from conducting business as usual. The latter action, called May Day by protesters, had been met with elite army troops occupying the nation's capital, and by large-scale unlawful detentions of thousands of demonstrators by police and security forces. A few days later, the American ambassador to South Vietnam blandly told an interviewer he foresaw the need for American advisers and combat aircraft for at least several more years.

The Truth Revealed

Into this climate the Pentagon Papers dropped like a huge stink bomb. Suddenly the hidden intentions of American policymakers, at least through 1968, and their own understandings of the real situation in the Vietnam War, stood revealed. Suddenly there was something with which Americans could compare what they had been told about the war. That was the essential purpose of the person who leaked the Pentagon Papers. Daniel Ellsberg had worked in the Office of the Secretary of Defense during the Johnson years, had spent two years in Vietnam as a civilian analyst, numbered among the authors of the Pentagon Papers, and had since gone on to the RAND Corporation, a private think tank that worked closely with the U.S. military. Ellsberg felt mortified at the way the American public had been misled on Vietnam and thought that some-how prosecution of the war would become impossible if its shaky real underpinnings were revealed to public scrutiny. The blinding light of truth would end the war. It was Ellsberg who stood behind the articles that appeared in the *New York Times* on June 13, 1971. . . .

The Pentagon Papers were created as a top-secret project within the Department of Defense . . . but they came to the attention of the American people by virtue of the very frustra-tions and intense controversies just outlined. The vehicle for doing that was a leak. For a multitude of reasons, not least be-cause the primary sources of leaks are government officials themselves, leakers almost never acknowledge their actions. In this case, the source of the Pentagon Papers leak acknowl-edged his role days after the papers' first appearance in the press. Daniel Ellsberg within four years had been brought to the stark place where he saw revealing them as a measure that might help end the Vietnam War. The fact of the leak, and the right of the American people to learn of the contents of the Pentagon Papers, would be the main focus of the legal actions by the U.S. government against the media. . . .

A well-known defense analyst, Ellsberg had worked on nuclear weapons strategy and counterinsurgency theory. He had been in and out of the RAND Corporation, a think tank largely funded at the time by the U.S. Air Force, and had worked for the Office of the Secretary of Defense. There, the assistant secretary for international security affairs, John T. McNaughton, had brought Dr. Ellsberg on board in August 1964, the same day that U.S. warships in the Gulf of Tonkin claimed to have been attacked a second time by the North Vietnamese; that claim was used as the basis for a bombing raid on the North. Though the naval commander on the scene followed up his original report with cables expressing doubts, so that the reality of the attack stood in question from the first moments, Washington confidently asserted its charges against Hanoi and went ahead with the attack. (Today this second Gulf of Tonkin incident, on August 4, 1964, is believed not to have occurred.) Ellsberg was struck by the discrepancies between the U.S. government's private knowledge and its public statements. Repeatedly observing similar episodes, he came to believe that Washington was conducting the Vietnam War by systematically deceiving the American people.

In the summer of 1965, as the Johnson administration committed the nation to full-scale war, sending troops to fight on the ground in South Vietnam, Ellsberg did his part by volunteering for a mission that was intended to monitor the progress of the war right in the field, for which he transferred to State Department employment roles and worked under Edward G. Lansdale, a retired air force officer and CIA operative with long connections in South Vietnam. For two years Ellsberg put his doubts aside and worked to improve the efficiency of the war effort in Vietnam. Different misgivings grew during this period, as Ellsberg saw the United States unable to adopt proper tactics for the war it was fighting, and unwilling to draw appropriate political conclusions regarding the forces in South Vietnamese society that made Saigon an ineffective ally. Nevertheless Dr. Ellsberg worked hard, argued forcefully, and ended up as the special assistant to the deputy U.S. ambassador in charge of all pacification programs. Toward the end of that time, Ellsberg contracted hepatitis and had to return to the United States.

Growing Misgiving

A defining moment came in October 1966, when Ellsberg hitched a ride on a plane bringing defense secretary Robert S. McNamara back from one of his periodic inspection visits to South Vietnam. During the long plane ride home, McNamara called Ellsberg over to adjudicate an argument he was having with Robert Komer, then White House pacification chief, where McNamara took the line that the war situation was worse than it had ever been. Ellsberg then saw McNamara emerge from the plane when it landed at Andrews Air Force Base to tell reporters that Vietnam trends were much improved and he was greatly encouraged. Witnessing this episode rekindled Ellsberg's fears of government lying.

Daniel Ellsberg's Vietnam tour ended just after Secretary McNamara had ordered the creation of the Pentagon Papers study. He returned to Washington to complete the process of leaving government service and used the visit to carry his message of troubles in Vietnam to anyone who would listen. Dr. Ellsberg spent an hour with Robert McNamara, who he discovered was trying to rein in the ineffective bombing campaign over North Vietnam, and had an appointment with presidential national security adviser Walt W. Rostow, who proved completely impervious to any assertion that the Vietnam situation was other than good (and getting better). Ellsberg's views had little impact as he warned of unalterable stalemate in Vietnam and impending deterioration of the U.S. position, but he carried the word to Pentagon science advisers, groups of media executives, even to then-Senator Robert F. Kennedy.

An Insider View

Ellsberg's ultimate destination was the RAND Corporation, again, but there would be another detour through Washington. Dan knew several of the senior officials coordinating the Pentagon Papers effort. As a long-service defense analyst with considerable Vietnam experience, Ellsberg was a natural choice to work on the study and he figured among the early hires. Seconded from RAND to the Office of the Secretary of Defense, Dan Ellsberg spent months reviewing the record of the CIA's intelligence estimates on Vietnam, as well as studying the decisions made by President John Kennedy. A draft for this portion of the study would be Ellsberg's contribution to the Pentagon Papers. Still consulting for RAND at the Pentagon early in 1968 when North Vietnam and the National Liberation Front unleashed their countrywide Tet Offensive, Ellsberg saw the top-secret recommendations to send more American troops to Vietnam that flowed from senior commanders. The RAND analyst was less shocked at the offensive than by the demands it triggered. Generals told Congress that nuclear weapons would be used in South Vietnam if required to save one American base under siege. The Joint Chiefs of Staff used the occasion to ask for massive reinforcements, 206,000 troops, the exact number they had requested (but had been turned down by President Johnson) in early 1967, in effect pressing their case for U.S. national mobilization. The reinforcement scheme foundered after word of it leaked to the newspapers. By his own account this taught Dan Ellsberg that presidents' ability to escalate the war had depended upon secrecy and the ability to avoid disclosures of their strategy.

The Tet Offensive that engulfed South Vietnam early in 1968 turned Dan Ellsberg very strongly against the Vietnam War. He became a frequent participant at conferences on Vietnam, including ones sponsored by the antiwar movement, and completed his evolution into a vocal opponent of U.S. involvement. Unlike other historians or Vietnam analysts, however, Ellsberg knew of the existence of the Pentagon Papers, which showed from the government's own secret files how its decisions had been made on faulty grounds from the very earliest stages of the war. Government secrecy, in Ellsberg's view, had functioned to perpetuate and escalate a policy that was damaging larger U.S. interests (he himself would later characterize this even more starkly as genocidal).

Leaking the Report

Americans thought they were voting for peace in Vietnam in the 1968 election that brought to power Richard M. Nixon. By then negotiations on a settlement and U.S. withdrawal from South Vietnam had begun. As part of the Nixon presidential transition, newly minted National Security Adviser Henry A. Kissinger decided to conduct a policy review on the Vietnam War and engaged the RAND Corporation to write an options paper and an associated study that could identify the differences among U.S. agencies on progress (or the lack thereof) in Vietnam. Among Dr. Ellsberg's final tasks for the U.S. government was to compile the set of questions used in this study and do the initial draft of the options paper. Ellsberg later helped assemble the agency responses to the questionnaire. Kissinger aide Winston Lord wrote most of the summary report that analyzed the material, in collaboration with Ellsberg and Morton H. Halperin, another Kissinger aide, as well as a former McNamara Pentagon official. In the course of this work, Ellsberg learned that the Nixon administration policy paper had been revised to drop the option for an American withdrawal from South Vietnam. The option for an attempt to win the war had been kept. When the Nixon administration's secret bombing of Cambodia was revealed, followed by its invasion of that country in 1970 and then of Laos in 1971, it seemed as if the win-the-war strategy was the one in play. Dan Ellsberg went into public dissent in October 1969 when he and five other senior analysts at RAND sent an open letter opposing the Vietnam War that was published in the *Washington Post*.

Dan Ellsberg's path to leaking the Pentagon Papers began then. In the first part of 1969, he read the full text of the massive Pentagon Papers, a set of which was held in storage at RAND. Around the time of the letter incident, Ellsberg determined to somehow use the McNamara study of the war to influence the course of events. Dr. Ellsberg's initial idea was to get the document to Congress and use it as the focus for intense investigative hearings that could expose the real history of the war. That required having a copy of the documents he could show around to enlist supporters. Ellsberg went to a friend and former RAND colleague, Anthony Russo, who was in full agreement with any measures that could help stop the Vietnam War. Russo, if anything more militant than Ellsberg, arranged for the use of a photocopying machine and helped Ellsberg make actual copies of the Pentagon Papers. With more help from Ellsberg's children, eventually reproductions of forty-three of the forty-seven volumes of the Pentagon Papers were made.

Efforts to Build Congressional Support

Dan Ellsberg's next move was to begin soliciting allies. During a November 1969 visit to Washington, he saw the powerful chairman of the Senate Foreign Relations Committee, J. William Fulbright, who was known to be angry at the way his legislative unit had been deliberately misled by the Johnson administration at the time of the Gulf of Tonkin incidents in 1964. Fulbright wanted to help but thought the way to go would be to get the Nixon administration to provide the Pentagon study through official channels. He therefore wrote to Defense Secretary Melvin R. Laird requesting the documents on November 8, 1969. Laird replied just before Christmas that the Pentagon would furnish the Congress with information about U.S. policies in Vietnam, but not with the Pentagon Papers, which he asserted had been constructed from contributions provided on the basis of promises of confidentiality. Senator Fulbright renewed his demand for the documents in late January 1970, and Laird waited more than six months before rejecting it that summer. In April 1971, just prior to the massive demonstrations that protested the Laotian invasion, Fulbright sent a third request for release of the Pentagon Papers. In the meantime the Senate Foreign Relations Committee had Dr. Ellsberg come before them as a witness at least two times.

None of this informed the American people as Ellsberg wished to do. At the hearings, without documents, the participants could only speak generally of U.S. policies. Fulbright made no open use of the Pentagon study, several thousand pages of which by now resided in the committee's vault. In 1970 again, Ellsberg also approached California congressman Ron Dellums, who brought staff aide Michael Duberstein along to a lunch where Ellsberg did not seem so certain of his course. Toward the end of that year and into the next winter, however, Dr. Ellsberg was in contact with South Dakota senator George S. McGovern (who would be the eventual Democratic Party candidate for president in 1972) in a fresh effort to get out the documents, but McGovern did not bite. The senator later told others he saw Ellsberg as a Vietnam hawk with a bad conscience. Ellsberg remembers his exchange with McGovern as being very positive, but that they never discussed the reasons when the senator backed away a week later from the initial commitment he made to filibuster with the Pentagon Papers.

Dan Ellsberg came to the fourth estate by this indirection. After failing with Congress, he began to reach out to writers and journalists. He provided some materials from the Pentagon Papers to Marcus Raskin, Richard Barnett, and Ralph Stavins of the Institute for Policy Studies (IPS). They were at work on a project that became the book *Washington Plans an Aggressive War*, which showed U.S. policy in Vietnam as lurching into war through blind resort to coercive diplomacy. Neither the IPS analysts nor anyone else received any of the four volumes of the Pentagon Papers that dealt with U.S. attempts to open negotiations with Hanoi. In March 1971 Ellsberg gave most of the Pentagon Papers text to reporter Neil Sheehan of the *New York Times*. . . .

During the heat of the court proceedings on the injunctions with which the Nixon administration prohibited the American press from publishing the Pentagon Papers, the government made claims as to the damage to U.S. national security that would be made by any disclosure of the secret government study, which was composed of a narrative portion with related documents attached as exhibits. Today the same kinds of claims about effects on U.S. security are made every day by government agencies responding to requests for release of records under the Freedom of Information Act (FOIA). This is a vital and continuing aspect of the operation of the FOIA system in the United States. The Pentagon Papers are the biggest and most detailed example that exist to this day of exactly how the U.S. government constructs arguments about damage to national security in the cases of records sought under FOIA. . . .

It is a revealing fact that in past and present decisions on releasing materials to the American public, publication in the Pentagon Papers has been used by government officials as a reason to release, but the Pentagon Papers themselves *remain secret to this day.* This is despite the existence in the public record of the Senator Mike Gravel edition of the Pentagon Papers (which consists of virtually the entire text of the forty-three volumes that formed part of the 1971 leak), as well as a Nixon administration-authorized version of the same documents that was printed by the House Armed Services Committee. An early 1990s FOIA request for the Pentagon Papers also, we are informed, was "lost" somewhere in the judge advocate general's office of the Department of Defense. At this writing, *three years* since one of the editors [of this essay] applied anew under the relevant provisions of FOIA, and more than *three decades* since the actual documents were already in the public domain, the U.S. government continues to hold the originals of the Pentagon Papers in its top-secret vaults. This is true even though the Vietnam War is over, the South Vietnamese government we supported no longer exists, the records themselves are of obvious historical value, and the applicable government regulations on declassification (a presidential executive order issued by Bill Clinton and modified by George W. Bush) specifies that government documents should be released after twenty-five years. The four volumes that Ellsberg withheld in 1971, the ones that concerned diplomatic negotiations that were deemed too sensitive at the time, were released in expurgated form in the 1980s to Morton H. Halperin and to George Herring, and finally in their full text under our FOIA request in May 2002. But the previously leaked material is still secret.

However arbitrary the U.S. government's treatment of the formerly secret (but in fact well-known) Pentagon Papers may appear, every American should understand that this represents the norm, not any aberration, in the operation of the declassification system. Examples of the excessive secrecy encouraged by the system range from the merely arbitrary to the completely absurd. . . .

The entire problem has only been magnified by the consequences of the events of September 11, 2001. Officials in doubt are now enjoined to keep records secret rather than release them, where the opposite predisposition had applied before, and the government is recalling documents previously declassified on the supposition that the records could somehow aid terrorists. For example, in navy records, documents on tankers sunk in the North Atlantic by German submarines during World War II have been reclassified on the grounds they have relevance to current U.S. national security.

Continuing growth and deepening of patterns of government secrecy is coupled with strong temptation on the part of government to preserve that secrecy by the abridgment of individual and constitutional rights, exactly as the Nixon administration attempted in the Pentagon Papers case. The attempt to impose prior restraint on the press and prevent the appearance in the media of material drawn from the Pentagon Papers, had it succeeded, would have given government the ability to avoid disclosure in any subsequent situation in which its actions were in question, were embarrassing, or where calling them into question was simply judged politically inconvenient by some executive. This is why the story of the Pentagon Papers, and what followed when Daniel Ellsberg leaked them, are of key importance for Americans today.

National Security Is More Important than Liberty in the War on Terror

Richard A. Posner

Richard A. Posner is a federal judge, a law professor, and the author of many books on U.S. law, including Economic Analysis of Law, The Problematics of Moral and Legal Theory. *He objects to civil libertarians who argue that freedoms should never be compromised in the name of national security. Americans should expect a reduction of their civil liberties during times of national crisis such as the aftermath of the September 11, 2001, terrorist attacks, he writes. Posner asserts that civil liberties such as freedom of speech and freedom from unreasonable arrest are always balanced by the relative need for safety during particular historical circumstances: National security should take precedence when the United States is threatened in any way, and civil liberty should take precedence during times of peace and prosperity.*

In the wake of the September 11 terrorist attacks have come many proposals for tightening security; some measures to that end have already been taken. Civil libertarians are troubled. They fear that concerns about national security will lead to an erosion of civil liberties. They offer historical examples of supposed overreactions to threats to national security. They treat our existing civil liberties—freedom of the press, protections of privacy and of the rights of criminal suspects, and the test—as sacrosanct, insisting that the battle against international terrorism accommodate itself to them.

I consider this a profoundly mistaken approach to the question of balancing liberty and security. The basic mistake

Richard A. Posner, "The Truth About Our Liberties," *Rights vs. Public Safety After 9/11: America in the Age of Terrorism.* Edited by Amitai Etzioni and Jason H. Marsh. Lanham, MD: Rowman & Littlefield, 2003. Reproduced by permission.

is the prioritizing of liberty. It is a mistake about law and a mistake about history. Let me begin with law. What we take to be our civil liberties—for example, immunity from arrest except upon probable cause to believe we've committed a crime and from prosecution for violating a criminal statute enacted after we committed the act that violates it—were made legal rights by the Constitution and other enactments. The other enactments can be changed relatively easily, by amendatory legislation. Amending the constitution is much more difficult. In recognition of this, the framers left most of the constitutional provisions that confer rights pretty vague. The courts have made them definite.

Prioritizing Safety

Concretely, the scope of these rights has been determined, through an interaction of constitutional text and subsequent judicial interpretation, by a weighing of competing interests. I'll call them the public-safety interest and the liberty interest. Neither, in my view, has priority. They are both important, and their relative importance changes from time to time and from situation to situation. The safer the nation feels, the more weight judges will be willing to give to the liberty interest. The greater the threat that an activity poses to the nation's safety, the stronger will the grounds seem for seeking to repress that activity even at some cost to liberty. This fluid approach is only common sense.

If it is true, therefore, that the events of September 11 have revealed the United States to be in much greater jeopardy from international terrorism than had previously been believed—have revealed it to be threatened by a diffuse, shadowy enemy that must be fought with police measures as well as military force—it stands to reason that our civil liberties will be curtailed. They should be curtailed, to the extent that the benefits in greater security outweigh the costs in reduced liberty. All that can reasonably be asked of the responsible legislative and judicial officials is that they weigh the costs as carefully as the benefits.

It will be argued that the lesson of history is that officials habitually exaggerate dangers to the nation's security. But the lesson of history is the opposite. It is because officials have repeatedly and disastrously underestimated these dangers that our history is as violent as it is. Consider such underestimated dangers as that of secession, which led to the Civil War; of a Japanese attack on the United States, which led to the disaster at Pearl Harbor; of Soviet espionage in the 1940s, which accelerated the Soviet Union's acquisition of nuclear weapons and emboldened Stalin to encourage North Korea's invasion of South Korea; of the installation of Soviet missiles in Cuba, which precipitated the Cuban missile crisis; of political assassinations and outbreaks of urban violence in the 1960s; of the Tet Offensive of 1968; of the Iranian revolution of 1979 and the subsequent taking of American diplomats as hostages; and, for that matter, of the events of September 11.

Better to Err on the Side of Caution

It is true that when we are surprised and hurt, we tend to overreact—but only with the benefit of hindsight can a reaction be separated into its proper and excess layers. In hindsight we know that interning Japanese Americans did not shorten World War II. But was this known at the time? If not, shouldn't the Army have erred on the side of caution, as it did? Even today we cannot say with any assurance that Abraham Lincoln was wrong to suspend *habeas corpus* during the Civil War, as he did on several occasions, even though the Constitution is clear that only Congress can suspend this right. (Another of Lincoln's wartime measures, the Emancipation Proclamation, may also have been unconstitutional.) But Lincoln would have been wrong to cancel the 1864 presidential election, as some urged: By November 1864, the North was close to victory, and canceling the election would have created a more dangerous precedent than the wartime suspension of habeas corpus. This last example shows that civil liberties remain part of the balance even in the most dangerous of times and even though their relative weight must then be less.

Lincoln's unconstitutional acts during the Civil War show that even legality must sometimes be sacrificed for other values. We are a nation under law, but first we are a nation. I want to emphasize something else, however: the malleability of law, its pragmatic rather than dogmatic character. The law is not absolute, and the slogan *"Fiat iustitia rat caelum "* (Let justice be done though the heavens fall) is dangerous nonsense. The law is a human creation rather than a divine gift, a tool of government rather than a mandarin mystery. It is an instrument for promoting social welfare, and as the conditions essential to that welfare change, so must it change.

The "War on Drugs" and Civil Liberties

Civil libertarians today are missing something else—the opportunity to challenge other public-safety concerns that impair civil liberties. I have particularly in mind the war on drugs. The sale of illegal drugs is a "victimless" crime in the special but important sense that it is a consensual activity. Usually there is no complaining witness, so in order to bring the criminals to justice, the police have to rely heavily on paid informants (often highly paid and often highly unsavory), undercover agents, wiretaps and other forms of electronic surveillance, elaborate sting operations, the infiltration of suspect organizations, random searches, the monitoring of airports and highways, the "profiling" of likely suspects on the basis of ethnic or racial identity or national origin, compulsory drug tests, and other intrusive methods that put pressure on civil liberties.

The war on drugs has been a big flop; moreover, in light of what September 11 has taught us about the gravity of the terrorist threat to the United States, it becomes hard to take entirely seriously the threat to the nation that drug use is said to pose. Perhaps it is time to redirect law enforcement resources from the investigation and apprehension of drug deal-ers to the investigation and apprehension of international ter-rorists. By doing so we may be able to minimize the net decrease in our civil liberties that the events of September 11 have made inevitable.

Freedom from Censorship Is Crucial in the Age of Terrorism

Daniel P. Tokaji

In the following selection Daniel P. Tokaji argues that during times of national crisis, providing opportunities for citizens to register their views about government policies is essential in preserving a healthy democracy. After the terrorist attacks of September 11, 2001, few Americans engaged in public debate about the federal government's War on Terror, military intervention in Afghanistan, and domestic policies such as the Patriot Act, which limited civil liberties defined in the Bill of Rights, Tokaji writes. He states that he believes the reason public debate has been relatively sparse is because citizens do not have enough oppourtunities to participate in the democracy. Tokaji also asserts that the government needs to provide more possibilities for such public debate, which is necessary in a just society. In order to allow open dissent against its own policies, the government should support nonprofit organizations and adopt national service programs that encourage citizens to work in the nonprofit sector, including nonprofit organizations that oppose government policies, Tokaji writes.

Tokaji worked as a staff attorney at the American Civil Liberties Union Foundation of Southern California and is a professor at the Moritz College of Law at the Ohio State University in Columbus.

It is perhaps unsurprising that in the immediate aftermath of the September 11 attacks, the nation witnessed a dearth of public dissent. The horrifying assaults upon citadels of

American economic and military strength, combined with the anguish of seeing so many innocent people killed, created an apparent national unity not witnessed in decades.

Somewhat more surprising than the initial wave of post-September 11 unity is how little dissent accompanied public policy debates in the months that followed, despite growing reasons to question American policy both at home and abroad. A broad consensus of public opinion, to be sure, supported military intervention in Afghanistan, the initial phase of the so-called War Against Terror. But with the Taliban vanquished and the Al-Qaeda network disrupted if not destroyed, a number of difficult policy questions have emerged. Who exactly *are* our enemies in the War on Terror? How long can this war be expected to persist? How will we know when it ends? Is it appropriate for the United States preemptively to strike Iraq or other nations, based on the mere possibility of future terrorist acts?

Equally vital questions lie before us on the domestic front, some of which are being explored in the other chapters to this volume. For example, as our temporal distance from September 11 increases, will Americans be willing to tolerate the incursions upon our privacy and other civil liberties that John Ashcroft's Justice Department insists are necessary? Is it appropriate for the government to deport noncitizens based on mere suspicion of ties to groups that the government has deemed terrorist organizations? To what extent must the traditional wall of separation between foreign intelligence-gathering activities (traditionally conducted by the CIA) and domestic law enforcement activities (traditionally conducted by the FBI) be abrogated in order to ensure domestic security? And while attention is focused on the War on Terror, must we push to the back burner domestic issues, such as a faltering economy and the torrent of corporate scandals that came to light as the nation was reeling from September 11? To what extent does responsibility for these crises lie with the federal government, including the legislators from both major parties who received large contributions from those linked to the wave of corporate malfeasance?

This [selection] endeavors not to answer these questions but instead to inquire into the reasons for our impoverished public discourse regarding them. My thesis is that the relative scarcity of public dissent over American foreign and domestic policy in the early stages of this age of terrorism reflects a deeper problem in American democracy, one that challenges conventional First Amendment doctrine. More specifically, I argue that the dearth of dissent in the wake of September 11—and the accompanying disinterest in politics on the part of the American public—is a product of the inadequacy of opportunities for citizen participation in the life of democracy. Despite the proliferation of outlets for communication, such as cable stations and Internet sites, we lack the sort of "robust, uninhibited and wide-open" public debate that Justice Brennan's opinion in *New York Times v. Sullivan* envisioned. Perhaps the best evidence of the poor condition of our political discourse is the abysmal rate of voter turnout, especially among people of color. Equally telling is the silence of our government in response to the question "What can I do for my country?," which many Americans found themselves asking in the days after September 11. The absence of a coherent answer to this question suggests that our political and legal institutions have failed to create the opportunities for citizen participation that post-September 11 democracy demands.

Negative Equality vs. Positive Equality

At least partly to blame for our impoverished discourse, I argue, are the inadequacies of contemporary First Amendment doctrine. That doctrine is designed to prevent state officials from intentionally suppressing disfavored messages or ideas and is quite well-suited to accomplish this end. Indeed, it is largely because of the doctrine's strength in this regard that

149

post-September 11 America has, for the most part, been spared McCarthy-style tactics aimed at silencing dissenting voices. While this *laissez faire* approach may prevent government from actively suppressing speech, it is not sufficient to ensure a robust marketplace of competing ideas. The inadequacies of this *laissez faire* approach to speech become especially apparent, where private rather than governmental entities limit channels for dissemination of dissenting viewpoints and where economic inequalities limit speakers' abilities to make themselves heard. Put another way, existing free speech doctrine is designed to safeguard "negative equality," by which I mean the state's affirmative suppression of unpopular views; but is not designed to advance "positive equality" by increasing the opportunities for all citizens to participate in public discourse.

This [selection] argues that the scarcity of dissent in the wake of September 11 reflects a serious First Amendment problem, the solution to which must include promotion of positive equality and, more specifically, the creation of pathways though which citizens of limited means may participate in the life of democracy. One such reform would be the creation of a more robust program of national service that includes opportunities for advocacy of political issues. In explaining why the government should play a role in stimulating political activism on the part of its citizens, I turn to what might seem unlikely sources: Dr. Martin Luther King's "Letter from Birmingham City Jail" and the philosophy of dissent that he borrows from Henry David Thoreau's classic essay "Civil Disobedience." Both men wrote about the centrality of dissent in times of great moral crisis, and our existing national service legislation expressly cites King's "life and teachings" as a source of inspiration. Yet the modest national service program that currently exists fails to adequately embody his vision of citizen activism, including its importance both to the individual's moral life and to a healthy democratic discourse. An enhanced federally funded program that included an advocacy component would, I argue, serve both these ends. It would encourage participation by those who until now have not been engaged citizens and would promote a more vibrant democracy. . . .

In explaining the importance of both negative and positive equality. I turn to two seminal essays explaining the necessity of dissent in times of crisis. Henry David Thoreau's "Civil Disobedience" depicts dissent as a moral obligation, taking the position that the individual has a responsibility to speak out—and even to disobey the law—in opposition to an unjust system of government. Martin Luther King, Jr.'s "Letter from Birmingham City Jail" turns Thoreau's philosophy of civil disobedience toward political strategy, explaining its use as a tactic by which to end racial segregation. For both, dissent is an individual moral obligation as well as a step toward the elimination of existing injustices. King and Thoreau's writings thus explain the necessity of dissent to the health of the individual and to democracy. They also bring into focus the inadequacy of existing institutions, manifest in the scarcity of dissent in post-September 11 public discourse, in terms of their failure to promote positive speech equality.

King wrote "Letter from Birmingham City Jail" in April 1963 while serving a sentence for participation in civil rights demonstrations, the same set of demonstrations that would, six years later, give rise to the Supreme Court's decision in *Shuttlesworth v. Birmingham*. King's open letter was addressed to eight prominent white clergymen who had criticized the Birmingham demonstrations as "unwise and untimely" and urged that the struggle for integration be allowed to proceed through the judicial system. The letter attempts to explain the reasons for adopting direct action tactics, such as public demonstrations and marches, that contravened local laws.

Civil Disobedience

King's letter serves as a powerful affirmation of a radical form of dissent, civil disobedience, both to the individual confronted with serious injustice and to a healthy democracy. King begins his justification of the demonstrators' illegal actions by distinguishing between just and unjust laws, characterizing segregation as a form of the latter. He further explains that laws such as Birmingham's permit statute may be "just on their face and unjust in its application," insofar as it is used to "preserve segregation and deny citizens the First Amendment privilege of peaceful assembly." While the clergy to whom the letter was responding viewed the "tension" caused by his demonstrations as a bad thing, King explains that such tension is vital in order to tear down an unjust system. He unfavorably contrasts the "negative peace"—the absence of public dissent urged by the white clergy—with the "positive peace which is the presence of justice." The need to advance such a positive peace, according to King, justified peaceful demonstrations that violated the laws of the City of Birmingham. Indeed, violation of the law constituted a critical part of the demonstrations' expressive impact, since it focused attention on conditions that would otherwise have gone unnoticed and unrepaired. Breaking the city's laws served as a powerful means by which to expose the unfairness of the system of racial segregation that Birmingham typified and thereby bring about the demolition of this unjust system.

Such demonstrations did not, however, merely serve the instrumental purpose of promoting a more just society; they also served a vital expressive function for the African Americans who were expressing their dissent: "The Negro has many pent-up resentments and latent frustrations. He has to get them out." This statement captures the duality of dissent: its importance both to the individual and to the objective of achieving societal change. Dissent fulfills a "vital urge" of the individual, providing a "creative outlet" for those long subject to oppression. It also serves the systemic interest of developing a more just democracy, which King describes as the "cosmic urgency toward the promised land of racial justice." These two purposes come together, insofar as individuals' participation in a collective effort to improve existing conditions is seen as a moral imperative. In using the term "imperative," I mean to suggest a Kantian moral aspect to King's defense of civil disobedience, something that is most directly suggested by his assertion that "there is no greater treason than to do the right deed for the wrong reason." Dissent not only serves a collective instrumental purpose, moving us toward a more just society, but also fulfills the individual's moral need to speak out against injustice.

Dissent Benefits the Individual and Society

In expressing the duality of dissent, its necessity both to the individual and to society, King self-consciously borrows from Thoreau's essay "Civil Disobedience." As Thoreau describes in this essay, he had refused to pay his poll tax as an act of dissent against American foreign and domestic policy—specifically, the then-ongoing war on Mexico and the institution of slavery—and willingly went to jail for his refusal to obey the laws of the Commonwealth of Massachusetts. Thoreau explains his actions as a "duty," just as King expresses the moral imperative of publicly expressing opposition to a system that is unjust to its very core. As Thoreau puts it, "[slavery's] very Constitution is evil," and he later complains of the "sanction which the Constitution gives to slavery." King's idea that there exists not only a moral right but also a moral obligation to express dissent when faced with an unjust system is drawn directly from Thoreau.

For both King and Thoreau, then, civil disobedience at once promotes the instrumental objective of creating a more just society and the individual's moral obligation to speak out against existing injustice. Moreover, both envision a democracy that not only tolerates but also encourages dissent, and thereby facilitates its own regeneration. In Thoreau's words:

I please myself with imagining a state at last which can afford to be just to all men, and to treat the individual with respect as a neighbor; which even would not think it inconsistent with its own repose if a few were to live aloof from it, not meddling with it nor embraced by it, who fulfilled the duties of neighbors and fellow-men. A State which bore this kind of fruit, and suffered it to drop off as fast as it ripened, would prepare the way for a still more perfect and glorious State, which I have also imagined, but not yet anywhere seen.

By "pleas[ing]" himself through imagining a more just state, Thoreau (like King) suggests that civil disobedience serves the needs of the individual. At the same time, the metaphor of a fruit dropping off the tree "as fast as it ripened" suggests the creation a "more perfect" state, one that would contain the seeds of renewal—that would not inhibit but instead encourage the sort of healthy tension that King understood as necessary to remedy existing injustice. Both King and Thoreau are of course most directly concerned with promoting racial equality, in Thoreau's case the abolition of slavery and in King's case the abolition of segregation. Yet implicit in both of their essays is also an ideal of how democracy should work. Part of this vision is, of course, the negative egalitarian idea that the government should allow speakers of various points of view to express themselves. It is not, however, sufficient that the state simply keep its hands off speakers seeking to express their own moral convictions; the state also has an affirmative obligation to "be just to all men." Both imagine a more perfect state, one that provides an outlet for individuals to express dissent and thereby contains the seeds of its own renewal. . . .

Our democracy is still a long way from this vision. Citizen engagement and participation are at historic lows, and dissent, if not affirmatively suppressed, is certainly not encouraged. The question thus to be asked is: Can we imagine something better? And might it be argued that the imperative for creation of something better lies in the Constitution itself?. . .

Encouraging Government Dissent

It might seem strange to suggest that the government should play a role in fostering dissent against its own policies. But the idea of government funding the speech of nonprofit organizations, including speech that seeks to challenge the government's own actions, is not as revolutionary as it might initially sound. This was, after all, one of the purposes served by federally funded legal services. Federal monies for legal services have long been used to fund litigation challenging the actions of the federal government—and, indeed, providing indigent persons with the means by which to challenge government action was one of the core objectives of the legal services program. Under *L.S.O. v. Velazquez*, moreover, the federal government is prohibited from imposing viewpoint-discriminatory conditions upon entities that receive federal legal services funds. While there is no enforceable constitutional requirement that Congress fund legal services for the indigent, to the extent that it chooses to do so, there is a limit on its ability to prevent entities receiving those monies from engaging in dissenting speech.

So too, there is no enforceable constitutional requirement that Congress advance positive equality through adoption of a national service program containing an advocacy component. While these are content-based restrictions upon the use of funds, they appear tailored to avoid viewpoint-based restriction upon the uses of government funds—which would likely be deemed unconstitutional under *Rosenberger* and *L.S.O. v. Velazquez*. If, for example, Congress were to allow Americorps funding to nonprofits that support the war in Iraq but prohibit it to groups that oppose that war, such a restriction would almost certainly violate the rule against viewpoint discrimination laid down in these cases.

Expansion of the national service program is only one example of how the ideal of positive equality in the realm of expansion might be advanced. Increasing the amount of funding for the nonprofit sector would enable individuals to participate in service activities that would include an advocacy component. It would thereby further King and Thoreau's vision of a more just state, one that contains the seeds of its own renewal. . . .

The premise of this [selection] is that the response to September 11 presents a serious First Amendment challenge, one that our existing institutions and doctrine are inadequate to meet. Its argument is that the political branches of government can and should do more to promote citizen engagement in the life of our democracy, and that enhancement of the existing national service program to include an advocacy component would be a step in the right direction. Such a component should allow funding for a wide range of viewpoints, including advocacy in opposition to actions of the national government. This would serve vital free speech interests, including both the individual's interest in self-expression and society's interest in a robust public discourse that includes antagonistic viewpoints. I do not of course mean to suggest that this proposal would be a panacea for the serious problems of citizen disengagement that plagues post-September 11 democracy. Expansion of the national service program to allow increased government support for nonprofit speech is, however, one way in which the government might seek to promote *New York Times v. Sullivan*'s vision of an "unfettered interchange of ideas for bringing about political and social changes desired by the people," a constitutional ideal that may not be not completely realizable but to which we can and should aspire.

The Patriot Act Violates Freedom of Speech

Nancy Kranich

In the aftermath of the September 11, 2001 terrorist attacks, the U.S. Congress passed several measures to strengthen national security, including the Patriot Act. Critics of the Patriot Act have objected to several of its sections that limit civil liberties defined in the Bill of Rights of the U.S. Constitution. Of particular concern are the sections that amend laws governing search and seizure procedure, gag orders, foreign intelligence, wiretapping, and immigration. In this selection Nancy Kranich, past president of the American Library Association (ALA), argues that the Patriot Act violates public librarians' and library patrons' right to privacy, intellectual freedom, and free speech. Kranich believes that act creates dangerous censorship during a time when information is crucial for Americans to participate responsibly in a democratic government. In response to the Patriot Act and other policies, some citizens and organizations have resisted by refusing to enforce what they consider the objectionable policies and have proposed countermeasures to protect civil liberites. Nancy Kranich wrote this essay as a senior research fellow for the Free Expression Policy Project.

[Editor's note: The most controversial provisions of the Patriot Act that Kranich objects to in this section were renewed by Congress in March 2006.]

Hours after the terrorist attacks on September 11, 2001, people rushed to libraries to read about the Taliban, Islam, Afghanistan and terrorism. Americans sought background materials to foster understanding and cope with this horrific event. They turned to a place with reliable answers—to a

Nancy Kranich, "The Impact of the USA PATRIOT Act on Free Expression," www.fep project.org, May 5, 2003. Reproduced by permission.

trustworthy public space where they are free to inquire, and where their privacy is respected.

Since 9-11, libraries remain more important than ever to ensuring the right of every individual to hold and express opinions and to seek and receive information, the essence of a thriving democracy. But just as the public is exercising its right to receive information and ideas—a necessary aspect of free expression—in order to understand the events of the day, government is threatening these very liberties, claiming it must do so in the name of national security.

The USA Patriot Act

While the public turned to libraries for answers, the Bush Administration turned to the intelligence community for techniques to secure U.S. borders and reduce the possibility of more terrorism. The result was new legislation and administrative actions that the government says will strengthen security. Most notably, Congress passed into law the "Uniting and Strengthening America by Providing Appropriate Tools Required to Intercept and Obstruct Terrorism Act" (USA Patriot Act) just six weeks after the events of September 11. This legislation broadly expands the powers of federal law enforcement agencies to gather intelligence and investigate anyone it suspects of terrorism.

The USA Patriot Act contains more than 150 sections and amends over 15 federal statutes, including laws governing criminal procedure, computer fraud, foreign intelligence, wiretapping, and immigration. Particularly troubling to free speech and privacy advocates are four provisions: section 206, which permits the use of "roving wiretaps" and secret court orders to monitor electronic communications to investigate terrorists; sections 214 and 216, which extend telephone monitoring authority to include routing and addressing information for Internet traffic relevant to any criminal investigation; and, finally, section 215, which grants unprecedented authority to the Federal Bureau of Investigation (FBI) and other law enforcement agencies to obtain search warrants for business, medical, educational, library, and bookstore records merely by claiming that the desired records may be related to an ongoing terrorism investigation or intelligence activities—a very relaxed legal standard which does not require any actual proof or even reasonable suspicion of terrorist activity.

Equally troubling, section 215 includes a "gag order" provision prohibiting any person or institution served with a search warrant from disclosing what has taken place. In conjunction with the passage of the USA Patriot ACt, the U.S. Justice Department issued revised FBI guidelines in May 2002 that greatly increase the bureau's surveillance and data collection authority to access such information as an individual's Web surfing habits and search terms.

A Danger to Civil Rights

These enhanced surveillance powers license law enforcement officials to peer into Americans' most private reading, research, and communications. Several of the Act's hastily passed provisions not only violate the privacy and confidentiality rights of those using public libraries and bookstores, but sweep aside constitutional checks and balances by authorizing intelligence agencies (which are within the executive branch of government) to gather information in situations that may be completely unconnected to a potential criminal proceeding (which is part of the judicial branch of government). The constitutional requirement of search warrants, to be issued by judges, is one such check on unbridled executive power. In addition to the dangers to democracy from such unbridled executive power, it is not clear that these enhanced investigative capabilities will make us safer, for under the new provisions, far more reformation is going to the same intelligence agencies that were failing to manage the ocean of information they collected prior to September 11.

We do not know how the USA Patriot Act and related measures have been applied in libraries, bookstores, and other venues because the gag order bars individuals from making that information public. The executive branch has refused to answer inquiries from members of the House and Senate Judiciary Committees, and from civil liberties groups under the Freedom of Information Act, regarding the incidence of surveillance activities, except an admission of snooping in libraries by FBI agents.

Officially, librarians are not allowed to comment on FBI visits to examine library users' Internet surfing and book-borrowing habits. Unofficially, though, some details have surfaced. Two nationwide surveys conducted at the University of Illinois after September 11 found that more than 200 out of 1,500 libraries surveyed had turned over information to law enforcement officials. A March 2003 article in the *Hartford Courant* revealed that librarians in Fairfield and Hartford, Connecticut, were visited by the FBI, but only one case involved a search warrant. And an *FW Weekly* article on April 17, 2003, cited a case in New Mexico where a former public defender was arrested by federal agents and interrogated for five hours after using a computer at a Santa Fe academic library, apparently as a result of a chat room statement that President Bush was out of control. It is unclear whether any of these incidents involved secret search warrants as authorized under section 215 of the USA Patriot Act.

Federal officials claim that the USA Patriot Act and related measures have helped quash terrorist attacks. Mark Corallo, a Justice Department spokesman, has assured the public that, "We're not going after the average American. . . . If you're not a terrorist or a spy, you have nothing to worry about." Nevertheless, many American are uncomfortable relying on government officials for assurances that they will protect both civil liberties and national security effectively.

More Dangerous Policies

The USA Patriot Act is just one of several troubling policies that compromise the public's privacy rights. Another is the Enhanced Computer Assisted Passenger Pre-screening System (CAPPS-II), which profiles airline passengers and provides "No-Fly" watch lists to the Transportation Security Administration. The danger here is that all airline passengers are assigned a risk assessment "score" without recourse. As a result, innocent people could be branded security risks on the basis of flawed data and without any meaningful way to challenge the government's determination.

A third example is the Department of Defense Total Information Awareness program that seeks to scan billions of personal electronic financial, medical, communication, education, housing and travel transactions, analyze them utilizing both computer algorithms and human analysis, and then flag suspicious activity. Americans innocent of any wrongdoing could be targeted by this system because it will collect information (and misinformation) on everyone, much of which can be misused. Furthermore, a planned identity tracking system could follow individuals wherever they go.

And, finally, not to be overlooked, is the proposed "Domestic Security Enhancement Act of 2003," a more extreme version of the USA Patriot Act, which could be introduced in Congress at any time. This proposed legislation, leaked by a Justice Department official to the Center for Public Integrity, would make it easier for the government to initiate surveillance and wiretapping of U.S. citizens, repeal current court limits on local police gathering information on religious and political activity, allow the government to obtain credit and library records without a warrant, restrict release of information about health or safety hazards posed by chemical and other plants, expand the definition of terrorist actions to include civil disobedience, permit certain warrantless wiretaps and searches, loosen the standards for electronic eavesdropping of entirely domestic activity, and strip even native-born Americans of all of the rights of United States citizenship if they provide support to unpopular organizations labeled as terrorist by our government.

Resistance to Severe Limitations of Civil Rights

Citizens and organizations around the country are standing up and passing resolutions opposing the USA Patriot Act and related measures, and are urging local officials contacted by federal investigators to refuse requests that they believe violate civil liberties—whether Fourth Amendment rights to be free of unreasonable searches and seizures, First Amendment intellectual freedom and privacy rights, Fifth Amendment protections of due process, Sixth Amendment rights to a public trial by an impartial jury, Fourteenth Amendment equal protection guarantees, or the constitutional assurance of the writ of habeas corpus.

In addition, some in Congress are now leading legislative efforts to counter some of the more egregious provisions of the law. For instance, an alliance of librarians, booksellers, and citizen groups is working with Representative Bernie Sanders and more than 70 additional sponsors on the "Freedom to Read Protection Act of 2003." If passed, this Act would exempt libraries and bookstores from section 215 and would require a higher standard of proof than mere suspicion for search warrants presented at libraries and bookstores. Similarly, Senators Leahy, Grassley, and Specter have introduced the "Domestic Surveillance Act of 2003" to improve the administration and oversight of foreign intelligence surveillance.

Librarians and booksellers are counting on these efforts, along with public outcry, to stem federal actions that threaten Americans' most valued freedoms without necessarily improving national security. Until the protection of civil liberties reaches a balance with the protection of national security, libraries must affirm their responsibility to safeguard patron privacy by avoiding unnecessary creation and maintenance of personally identifiable information (PII) and developing up-to-date privacy policies that cover the scope of collection and retention of PII in data-related logs, digital records, vendor-collected data, and system backups, as well as more traditional circulation information. In short, if information is not collected, it cannot be released.

If libraries are to continue to flourish as centers for uninhibited access to information, librarians must stand behind their users' right to privacy and freedom of inquiry. Just as people who borrow murder mysteries are unlikely to be murderers, so those seeking information about Osama bin Laden are not likely to be terrorists. Assuming a sinister motive based on library users' reading choices makes no sense and leads to fishing expeditions that both waste precious law enforcement resources and have the potential to chill Americans' inquiry into current events and public affairs.

The millions of American who sought information from their libraries in the wake of September 11 reaffirm an enduring truth: a free and open society needs libraries more than ever. Americans depend on libraries to promote the free flow of information for individuals, institutions, and communities, especially in uncertain times. In the words of Supreme Court Justice William O. Douglas, "Restriction of free thought and free speech is the most dangerous of all subversions. It is the one un-American act that could most easily defeat us."

The Patriot Act Protects National Security and Civil Liberties

George W. Bush

George W. Bush is the forty-third president of the Unites States. This selection is an excerpt from a speech he delivered to the graduating class of the Ohio State Highway Patrol Academy in 2005. Bush argues in favor of renewing the Patriot Act in order to preserve national security. He declares that the act allows law enforcement access to information that helps fight terrorism on U.S. soil and abroad. By sharing data among law enforcement agencies, tracking phone conversations, and monitoring Internet communication criminal investigators are able to address terrorist threats before they result in tragedy. Bush asserts that the Patriot Act helps preserve the civil liberties of American citizens by establishing limits on law enforcement during investigations of terrorism.

My most solemn duty as President is to protect the American people. And I'm honored to share that responsibility with you. We have a joint responsibility. As sworn officers of the law, you're devoted to defending your fellow citizens. Your vigilance is keeping our communities safe, and you're serving on the front lines of the war on terror. It's a different kind of war than a war our nation was used to. You know firsthand the nature of the enemy. We face brutal men who celebrate murder, who incite suicide, and who would stop at nothing to destroy the liberties we cherish. You know that these enemies cannot be deterred by negotiations, or concessions, or appeals to reason. In this war, there's only one option—and that option is victory.

George W. Bush, "President Discusses Patriot Act," *The White House news release*, http://www.whitehouse.gov/news/releases/2005/2050609-2.html. The White House, June 9, 2005.

Since September the 11th, 2001, we have gone on the offensive against the terrorists. We have dealt the enemy a series of powerful blows. The terrorists are on the run, and we'll keep them on the run. Yet they're still active; they're still seeking to do us harm. The terrorists are patient and determined. And so are we. They're hoping we'll get complacent, and forget our responsibilities. Once again, they're proving that they do not understand our nation. The United States of America will never let down its guard.

Fighting Terrorism Abroad and at Home

This is a long war, and we have a comprehensive strategy to win it. We're taking the fight to the terrorists abroad, so we don't have to face them here at home. We're denying our enemies sanctuary, by making it clear that America will not tolerate regimes that harbor or support terrorists. We're stopping the terrorists from achieving the ideological victories they seek by spreading hope and freedom and reform across the broader Middle East. By advancing the cause of liberty, we'll lay the foundations for peace for generations to come.

And one of the great honors as the President is to be the Commander-in-Chief of a fantastic United States military— made fantastic by the quality and the character of the men and women who wear the uniform. Thank you for serving.

As we wage the war on terror overseas, we'll remember where the war began—right here on American soil. In our free and open society, there is no such thing as perfect security. To protect our country, we have to be right 100 percent of the time. To hurt us, the terrorists have to be right only once. So we're working to answer that challenge every day, and we're making good progress toward securing the homeland.

We've enhanced security at coastlines and borders and ports of entry. And we have more work to do. We've strengthened protections at our airports and chemical plants and highways and bridges and tunnels. And we got more work to do. We've made terrorism the top priority for law enforcement, and we've provided unprecedented resources to help folks like yourselves do their jobs.

Since 2001, we've more than tripled spending on homeland security, and we've increased funding more than tenfold for the first responders who protect our homeland. Law enforcement officers stand between our people and great dangers, and we're making sure you have the tools necessary to do your job.

The Purpose of the USA Patriot Act

We've also improved our ability to track terrorists inside the United States. A vital part of that effort is called the USA Patriot Act. The Patriot Act closed dangerous gaps in America's law enforcement and intelligence capabilities—gaps the terrorists exploited when they attacked us on September the 11th. Both houses of Congress passed the Patriot Act by overwhelming bipartisan majorities—98 out of 100 United States senators voted for the act. That's what we call bipartisanship. The Patriot Act was the clear, considered response of a nation at war, and I was proud to sign that piece of legislation.

Over the past three-and-a-half years, America's law enforcement and intelligence personnel have proved that the Patriot Act works, that it was an important piece of legislation. Since September the 11th, federal terrorism investigations have resulted in charges against more than 400 suspects, and more than half of those charged have been convicted. Federal, state, and local law enforcement have used the Patriot Act to break up terror cells in New York and Oregon and Virginia and in Florida. We've prosecuted terrorist operatives and supporters in California, in Texas, in New Jersey, in Illinois, and North Carolina and Ohio. These efforts have not always made the headlines, but they've made communities safer. The Patriot Act has accomplished exactly what it was designed to do—it has protected American liberty, and saved American lives.

Renewing the Patriot Act Is Critical

The problem is, at the end of this year [2005], 16 critical provisions of the Patriot Act are scheduled to expire. Some people call these "sunset provisions." That's a good name—because letting that—those provisions expire would leave law enforcement in the dark. All 16 provisions are practical, important, and they are constitutional. Congress needs to renew them all—and this time, Congress needs to make the provisions permanent.

We need to renew the Patriot Act because it strengthens our national security in four important ways. First, we need to renew the critical provisions of the Patriot Act that authorize better sharing of information between law enforcement and intelligence. Before the Patriot Act, criminal investigators were separated from intelligence officers by a legal and bureaucratic wall. A federal prosecutor who investigated Osama bin Laden in the 1990s explained the challenge this way: "We could talk to citizens, local police officers, foreign police officers—we could even talk to al Qaeda members. But there was one group of people we were not permitted to talk to—the FBI agents across the street from us assigned to parallel intelligence investigations of Osama Bin Laden and al Qaeda. That was a wall."

Allowing Access to Information

Finding our enemies in the war on terror is tough enough—law enforcement officers should not be denied vital information their own colleagues already have. The Patriot Act helped tear down this wall, and now law enforcement and intelligence officers are sharing information and working together, and bringing terrorists to justice.

In many terrorism cases, information-sharing has made the difference between success and failure—and you have an example right here in Columbus, Ohio. Two years ago, a truck driver was charged with providing support to al Qaeda. His capture came after an investigation that relied on the Patriot Act, and on contributions from more than a dozen agencies in the Southern Ohio Joint Terrorism Task Force. And members of that task force are with us today. I want to thank you for your contribution to the safety of America, and you'll understand this story I'm about to tell.

For several years, Iman Faris posed as a law-abiding resident of Columbus. But in 2000, he traveled to Afghanistan and met Osama bin Laden at an al Qaeda training camp. Faris helped the terrorists research airplanes and handle cash and purchase supplies. In 2002, he met Khalid Shaykh Muhammad—the mastermind of the September the 11th attacks— and he agreed to take part in an al Qaeda plot to destroy a New York City bridge.

After Faris returned to the United States, federal investigators used the Patriot Act to follow his trail. They used new information-sharing provisions to piece together details about his time in Afghanistan, and his plan to launch an attack on the United States. They used the Patriot Act to discover that Faris had cased possible targets in New York, and that he'd reported his findings to al Qaeda. In the spring of 2003, the FBI confronted Faris, and presented the case they had built against him. The case against him was so strong that Faris chose to cooperate, and he spent the next several weeks telling authorities about his al Qaeda association. Faris pled guilty to the charges against him. And today, instead of planning terror attacks against the American people, Iman Faris is sitting in an American prison.

The agents and prosecutors who used the Patriot Act to put Faris behind bars did superb work, and they know what a difference information-sharing made. Here is what one FBI agent said—he said, "The Faris case would not have happened without sharing information." That information-sharing was made possible by the Patriot Act. Another investigator on the case said, "We never would have had the lead to begin with."

You have proved that good teamwork is critical in protecting America. For the sake of our national security, Congress must not rebuild a wall between law enforcement and intelligence.

Providing Tools to Fight Terrorism

Second, we need to renew the critical provisions of the Patriot Act that allow investigators to use the same tools against terrorists that they already use against other criminals. Before the Patriot Act, it was easier to track the phone contacts of a drug dealer than the phone contacts of an enemy operative. Before the Patriot Act, it was easier to get the credit card receipts of a tax cheat than an al Qaeda bank-roller. Before the Patriot Act, agents could use wiretaps to investigate a person committing mail fraud, but not to investigate a foreign terrorist. The Patriot Act corrected all these pointless double standards—and America is safer as a result.

One tool that has been especially important to law enforcement is called a roving wiretap. Roving wiretaps allow investigators to follow suspects who frequently change their means of communications. These wiretaps must be approved by a judge, and they have been used for years to catch drug dealers and other criminals. Yet, before the Patriot Act, agents investigating terrorists had to get a separate authorization for each phone they wanted to tap. That means terrorists could elude law enforcement by simply purchasing a new cell phone. The Patriot Act fixed the problem by allowing terrorism investigators to use the same wiretaps that were already being using against drug kingpins and mob bosses. The theory here is straightforward: If we have good tools to fight street crime and fraud, law enforcement should have the same tools to fight terrorism.

Monitoring the Internet

Third, we need to renew the critical provisions of the Patriot Act that updated the law to meet high-tech threats like computer espionage and cyberterrorism. Before the Patriot Act, Internet providers who notified federal authorities about threatening e-mails ran the risk of getting sued. The Patriot Act modernized the law to protect Internet companies who voluntarily disclose information to save lives.

It's common sense reform, and it's delivered results. In April 2004, a man sent an e-mail to an Islamic center in El Paso, and threatened to burn the mosque to the ground in three days. Before the Patriot Act, the FBI could have spent a week or more waiting for the information they needed. Thanks to the Patriot Act, an Internet provider was able to provide the information quickly and without fear of a lawsuit—and the FBI arrested the man before he could fulfill his threat.

Terrorists are using every advantage they can to inflict harm. Terrorists are using every advantage of 21st century technology, and Congress needs to ensure that our law enforcement can use that same advantage, as well.

The Patriot Act Protects Civil Liberties

Finally, we need to renew the critical provisions of the Patriot Act that protect our civil liberties. The Patriot Act was written with clear safeguards to ensure the law is applied fairly. The judicial branch has a strong oversight role. Law enforcement officers need a federal judge's permission to wiretap a foreign terrorist's phone, a federal judge's permission to track his calls, or a federal judge's permission to search his property. Officers must meet strict standards to use any of these tools. And these standards are fully consistent with the Constitution of the U.S.

Congress also oversees the application of the Patriot Act. Congress has recently created a federal board to ensure that the Patriot Act and other laws respect privacy and civil liberties. And I'll soon name five talented Americans to serve on that board. Attorney General Gonzales delivers regular reports on the Patriot Act to the House and the Senate, and the Department of Justice has answered hundreds of questions from members of Congress. One Senator, Dianne Feinstein of California, has worked with civil rights groups to monitor my administration's use of the Patriot Act. Here's what she said: "We've scrubbed the area, and I have no reported abuses." Remember that the next time you hear someone make an unfair criticism of this important, good law. The Patriot Act has not diminished American liberties; the Patriot Act has helped to defend American liberties.

Every day the men and women of law enforcement use the Patriot Act to keep America safe. It's the nature of your job that many of your most important achievements must remain secret. Americans will always be grateful for the risks you take, and for the determination you bring to this high calling. You have done your job. Now those of us in Washington have to do our job. The House and Senate are moving forward with the process to renew the Patriot Act. My message to Congress is clear: The terrorist threats against us will not expire at the end of the year, and neither should the protections of the Patriot Act.

THE
HISTORY
OF
ISSUES

CHAPTER 4

Censorship Struggles in the Modern Cultural Arena

Chapter Preface

Some of the most contentious battles over censorship have been over popular culture, public forums, the arts, and libraries and schools. Two developments have greatly heightened these debates over freedom of speech: the countercultural movement of the 1960s and 1970s and the technological advances that accelerated in the 1980s and continue today.

During the 1960s, young people began to defy the numerous social conventions of earlier generations, including prohibitions against overt sexual expression and premarital sex. As the "sexual liberation movement" developed, many in the new generation of baby boomers—aided by innovations in contraception such as the birth control pill—claimed sexuality as an essential part of their identity and championed a new openness about sexual matters and relationships. The openness extended into popular and commercial culture, loosening proscriptions against forms of expression once deemed obscene.

Capitalizing on the demand for sexually explicit material, entrepreneurs built virtual empires of commercial pornography, such as *Playboy* and *Hustler*. However, these changes did not sit well with all Americans, and some publishers, such as Larry Flynt of *Hustler*, ended up in court cases defending pornography as a form of free speech. Moreover, the emerging women's liberation movement of the 1970s criticized the sexual exploitation of women and denounced most commercial pornography as sexist (although most feminists did not oppose other forms of erotica that they didn't consider a degradation of women's bodies). Meanwhile, while many artists had also pushed the boundaries of convention in earlier eras; vastly more painters, musicians, filmmakers, and writers of the counterculture movement were openly defying previous taboo—often with the support of the largest generation of people under thirty in U.S. history.

The countercultural movement of the 1960s and 1970s defied more than just sexual conventions: During that era, demonstrations against the Vietnam War sometimes included burning the American flag as a form of protest. Those who objected to public flag burnings passed the first federal Flag Protection Act in the U.S. Congress in 1968. Soon after, many states followed suit and passed their own legislation against flag desecration. However, the 1989 Supreme Court case *Texas v. Johnson* ultimately overturned all of these statutes, ruling that they were unconstitutional infringements on First Amendment protections of public expression. The controversy over whether flag desecration should be considered a form of free expression or a criminal act has continued into the new millennium.

Efforts to pass an amendment to the U.S. Constitution banning flag desecration gained new energy after the terrorist attacks of September 11, 2001. Arguments both for and against such an amendment often turn on clashing definitions of patriotism. For those in favor of criminalization, patriotism includes preserving the flag as a sacred symbol of the United States. For those who oppose criminalization, patriotism means preserving the civil liberties defined in the Bill of Rights—especially the freedom of expression.

The development of technologies such as the Internet has also greatly affected the debates over censorship. For example, as libraries and schools began have install computers for students in order to incorporate the Internet into educational activities, many Americans have become worried about young people accessing violent and pornographic content on the World Wide Web. Their concern led to the passage of the Children's Internet Protection Act (CIPA), which requires schools and libraries to protect minors from viewing violence, child pornography, and other obscene content while using computers with online access. This act, which was upheld by the Supreme Court in 2003, has spurred a great debate over what constitutes dangerous or obscene material that is worthy of censorship. In addition, some people have objected to the most popular method of protection—Internet filters—because they can sometimes exclude beneficial material along with harmful content.

As the new century continues to unfold, it is likely that further developments in the cultural and technological arenas will continue to spur many more debates over censorship in the world of art, politics, and popular culture.

With the passage of legislation such as the Patriot Act during the early twenty-first century war on terrorism, libraries have become a nexus of debate around issues of national security versus civil liberties. Americans argue over whether law enforcement should have access to the reading records of library patrons, records that before were protected as private in order to avoid the self-censorship of readers.

Outlawing Flag Desecration Is Dangerous Censorship

John S. Keating

Many attempts have been made to outlaw desecration of the American flag throughout U.S. history. All of the federal and state statutes were overturned by the Supreme Court of the United States in the 1989 case Texas v. Johnson. *In that case, laws against flag desecration were declared to be unconstitutional restrictions of freedom of expression. Since the* Texas v. Johnson *decision, lawmakers in support of flag protection have turned to the last remaining strategy to outlaw flag desecration by working to pass a flag protection amendment to the U.S. Constitution. This selection was written by attorney John S. Keating for the Freedom Forum, an organization that opposed a 1998 measure to amend the U.S. Constitution to prohibit flag desecration. Arguing that flag desecration is a protected form of political expression, Keating warns that legislation against it violates the spirit of the Bill of Rights, which is to constrain the power of the government, to protect unpopular speech, and to preserve basic human rights—especially the rights of those in the minority. For Keating, the symbolic meaning of the flag—representing liberty and democracy—is more important to preserve than any actual material flag.*

For 213 years, the Bill of Rights to the United States Constitution has stood as a barricade in defense of personal freedoms. Never in those two-plus centuries has this shining monument to the wisdom of our Founding Fathers been revised, much less diluted. In June 2003, the U.S. House of Representatives passed a measure that would inflict grievous harm upon the First Amendment within that Bill of Rights. The

U.S. Senate is poised to consider an identical measure, Senate Joint Resolution 4, some time before its adjournment this month.

This legislation proposes to grant Congress the power to prohibit the "desecration" of the American flag. If it passes the Senate by the required two-thirds majority (the vote is expected to be extremely close) and is later ratified by three-fourths of the states, it would become the 28th Amendment to the United States Constitution. For the following reasons, the Senate should reject this misguided and dangerous legislation.

The History and Purpose of the Bill of Rights

After establishing the framework for a democratic republic in the first seven articles of the Constitution, its proponents still faced significant opposition in a number of states. They soon realized that American suspicion of government was so strong that ratification of this new charter would require additional protections for the rights of individuals against governmental intrusion. What emerged was James Madison's brilliant Bill of Rights, with the protection of free speech being enshrined in the first of its ten amendments.

The Bill of Rights is purposefully anti-democratic, placing beyond the reach of transient political majorities those rights deemed as absolutely fundamental to the survival and prosperity of a free nation. Our Founding Fathers worried, correctly, that the politically weak and unpopular among us would otherwise fall prey to the passions and prejudices of our elected officials. Abraham Lincoln captured the essence of this idea in his first inaugural address, in which he stated: "If by sheer force of numbers a majority should deprive a minority of any clearly written constitutional right, it might, in a moral point of view, justify a revolution."

Thus, any popular support that this proposed amendment may enjoy—which results more from a revulsion at the act of flag desecration itself than from a dispassionate analysis of the measure's merits—should not serve as the basis for any Senator's vote in its favor. What is required of our Senators as they weigh the profound step of rewriting the Bill of Rights is to muster the wisdom and courage evidenced by their forebears and to put little stock in the latest polling data.

The Bill of Rights Constrains the Power of Government

The entire Bill of Rights is about limiting the power of government and securing our individual freedoms. The proposed amendment turns that principle on its head and would place constraints upon the political expression of the people. The only amendment to our constitution which has ever sought to deprive individual liberties is the Eighteenth, which imposed Prohibition. This measure was, of course, repealed only 14 years later by the 21st Amendment.

Freedom of speech, including symbolic speech, is one of the inalienable rights that our Declaration of Independence proclaimed significant enough to go to war. This freedom does not emanate from Congress. It is our birthright as U.S. citizens. Elected officials seldom like dramatic expressions of political dissent. Inherent in such dissent is criticism of those in power. Under Article I, Section 6 of the Constitution, members of Congress have absolute freedom to say whatever they like on the floor of either House—with no legal consequences, even for libeling an ordinary citizen. Yet, certain of these same elected officials would like to limit the people's First Amendment rights and put beyond the reach of reason or the courts the question of whether those in power can prohibit and punish the political speech of those not in power.

The First Amendment Protects Speech that Is Unpopular

The First Amendment was specifically designed to protect the expression of unorthodox views, unpopular ideas, and political dissent. Would it make any sense if it protected only orthodox views, popular ideas, and political harmony? Since when have these ever been in danger? Safe speech needs no guarantees of freedom, no Constitutional protection. The simple yet noble concept of "freedom of speech"—which has drawn so many asylum seekers and other immigrants to our shores over the centuries—would be rendered meaningless if it were limited to the expression of only those views deemed sufficiently agreeable or polite. As the Supreme Court stated in the 1943 case of *West Virginia vs. Barnette*, "No official, high or petty, can prescribe what shall be orthodox in politics, nationalism, religion or other matters of opinion . . ."

Our Founding Fathers were confident that the new nation they were forging would be vigorous enough to tolerate diversity and protect the rights of those expressing unpopular opinions. Indeed, that tolerance has served America well. As the United States Supreme Court noted in its opinion on the 1989 flag burning case of *Texas vs. Johnson*: "Our toleration of criticism such as Johnson's is a sign and source of our strength. Indeed, one of the proudest images of our flag, the one immortalized in our national anthem, is of the bombardment it survived at Fort McHenry. It is the nation's resilience, not its rigidity, that Texas sees reflected in the flag—and it is that resilience that we reassert today."

Vietnam Veteran Len Denney put it another way in a recent editorial: "If I must continue to tolerate, even protect the rights of people and beliefs that are repellent to my very soul, then so be it. It is a cheap price to pay for my freedom."

Desecration of the Flag Is a Form of Political Expression

Some say that flag desecration is merely an act, not a form of speech, and therefore deserves no protection under the First

Amendment. The Supreme Court held otherwise in *Texas vs. Johnson*, a ruling entirely consistent both with American history and common sense. Just as the flag is a symbol, so too is burning it a symbolic, albeit repugnant, form of expression. This, indeed, is the only possible purpose for such an act. . . .

Our forefathers were not unfamiliar with this concept. During the Revolutionary War, George Washington himself defaced a British flag by ordering 13 red and white stripes sewn on it. That desecrated flag was called "The Thirteen Rebellious Stripes." Similar actions were taken by both sides in the Civil War.

Other "mere acts" throughout our history have served as powerful, if distasteful, expressions of dissent. Vietnam War protesters burned not only flags but draft cards, and thereby helped foment debate on the wisdom of U.S. policy in Southeast Asia. Although they never uttered a word, the colonists who dumped British tea into Boston Harbor sent a message heard around the world.

The Substance Behind the Symbol Is What's Important

For over 200 years, the Constitution, and particularly the Bill of Rights, has governed the relationship between the government and the people, defining the powers of the former and the rights of the latter. It is, in short, an enunciation of the principles of freedom and democracy upon which our forebears founded this great nation. In this respect, it is profoundly unlike the flag which, however honored, is merely a symbol of those principles. The power of the flag is in its meaning, not its stitchery.

The many brave American soldiers who have died in combat did so defending the values represented by the flag, not the flag itself. One of the most important of these values is expressed in the First Amendment, which guarantees freedom of speech for all. As stated recently by Army veteran Keith A.

Kreul, Past National Commander of the American Legion: "American veterans who have protected our banner in battle have not done so to protect a 'golden calf.' Instead, they carried the banner forward with reverence for what it represents. . . . Therein lies the beauty of our flag."

The Bill of Rights Should Be Amended Under Only Compelling Circumstances

The Constitution is the "sacred text" of a nation forged upon the rule of law. Its ratification would not have been possible without the Bill of Rights, which has served since then as the single greatest instrument within the Constitution for securing the blessings of liberty enjoyed by generations of Americans. The Constitution is, quite simply, the most important document in our nation, and the Bill of Rights—emulated around the world, but whose freedoms are guarded no more jealously than where it arose—is its cornerstone. As such, those who would propose to tinker with it must be held to an exacting burden of proof, a proof that clearly demonstrates a compelling threat or need going to the fundamental structure of our national government. Of the 11,000 amendments proposed to our Constitution over two centuries, only 27 have been ratified—and none of these sought to narrow or limit a freedom guaranteed by the Bill of Rights.

The proposed amendment is, in stark contrast to this burden of proof, a solution in search of a problem if ever there was one. In the 227 years since the American flag was adopted, there have been fewer than 100 reported incidents of flag burning. The greatest concentration of these occurred during a five-year period, in the course of protests against the Vietnam War. Trifling with the Constitution and its Bill of Rights in response to a handful of flag burnings by a few misguided dolts would be overkill in the extreme. America is greater than that.

The primary purpose behind a protester's burning of the flag is to draw attention to his or her cause, however misguided. To make flag desecration a special exception to the First Amendment will only make it a more attractive form of protest. Instead of going to jail as a vandal, trespasser or riot inciter, a flag burner would be a political prisoner and a martyr to his or her cause. Whatever publicity one could gain by burning a flag would be magnified a hundredfold were this proposed amendment to become a part of the Constitution. Such a lure would be sure to subject veterans and other good citizens to the sorry spectacle of more flag burnings, not fewer.

"Compulsory Patriotism" Is Unworthy of a Free Nation

During an interrogation by one of his captors, Ivan Warner was shown a photograph of some Americans protesting the war by burning a flag. "People in your country protest against your cause. That proves you are wrong," said the North Vietnamese officer. "No," replied Warner, a Silver Star Medal and Purple Heart recipient. "That proves that I am right. In America, we are not afraid of freedom, even when we disagree." His answer enraged the North Vietnamese officer, giving Warner tremendous satisfaction at having turned the picture of the burning flag against his captor. "What better way to [respond]," Warner later observed about those who would burn the flag today, "Than with the subversive idea of freedom?"

In June 1998, less than a year after Hong Kong had been returned by Great Britain to the People's Republic of China, the Beijing-controlled legislature in Hong Kong outlawed the defacement of the Chinese flag. Other totalitarian regimes throughout history have sought solace by guarding their flags. Is this really the company we wish to keep? Black lists, loyalty oaths and other paranoid infringements of its citizens' civil liberties have been relegated to the dustbin of American history. We should not compromise our time-honored tradition of no-holds-barred political discourse to "save" a flag which has demonstrated its endurance through numerous wars, domestic unrest and other periods of great national stress. A truly free country has nothing to fear from free speech, even protest involving the desecration of the symbol of that freedom.

Beware the Slippery Slope

Virtually all of the Founding Fathers faced prison (or worse) because the government of the time found their speech to be offensive. They knew from first-hand experience how essential to a free society was the protection of even the most abhorrent and controversial of political expression. As Thomas Paine observed: "He that would make his own liberty secure, must guard even his enemy from oppression, for if he violates this duty, he establishes a precedent that will reach to himself." If one small voice can be silenced by amending the Constitution, it could happen to any or all of us. Do we really want to place in the hands of government the question of what constitutes "good" speech and what constitutes "bad" speech?

And if Congress is willing to tamper with the First Amendment today, what's to stop it from slicing and dicing the other nine parts of the Bill of Rights tomorrow? One footnote invites another. After the First Amendment comes the Second.

Respect for the Flag is Diminished, Not Enhanced, When the State Tries to Coerce It

"Old Glory" is the paramount symbol of the freedoms that Americans have treasured, and, in a great many cases, died for over more than two centuries. The profound esteem in which it already is held by the overwhelming majority of our 270 million citizens is far too great to be enhanced by criminalizing any gestures against it. What a terrible irony it would be, then, if for the first time in our history a portion of the Bill of

Rights is carved away under the guise of "saving" the flag. As the Supreme Court stated in *Texas vs. Johnson*: "We do not consecrate the flag by punishing its desecration, for in so doing we dilute the freedom that this cherished emblem represents."

The flag desecration amendment would not only eviscerate the First Amendment; it would also send a signal to the world of a nation unconfident of its citizens' allegiance and of its ability to endure criticism and dissent. Any additional measure of respect that might somehow be gained through threat of imprisonment would be neither earned nor deserved. If this measure were to pass, would we really be able to look upon the flag with quite as much pride and reverence as before?

Most acts of flag burning already are punishable under existing larceny, trespassing or public property statutes. The First Amendment allows punishment for acts of desecration performed in such a way as to incite a riot or produce a danger to others. All four persons who desecrated American flags in 1994, for example, were prosecuted under such statutes. Desecrating a flag that belongs to the government or to a nonconsenting individual is already punishable under the existing Federal Flag Code (4 USCA Sects. 1–10 [1998]).

Defining "Flag" and "Desecration" Is Difficult and Costly

Nowhere in the proposed amendment are the terms "flag" and "desecration" defined. The form of any statute Congress might pass were this measure to become a part of the Constitution is, at this point, anybody's guess. The American Heritage Dictionary (Second College Edition) defines "desecrate" as "to abuse the sacredness of." Not even the most ardent veterans groups argue that the flag is a religious icon. What kind or degree of disrespect might rise to the level of "desecration," particularly where the object in question—the American flag—is a secular symbol? Since burning is, under Title 36, Section 176(k) of the U.S. Code, the proper method for disposing of a worn flag, how would police and prosecutors determine which burnings are "proper" and which are not? Would any improper means of handling, storing or displaying a flag—Sections 174 through 176 of Title 36 contain 171 lines regulating these subjects—constitute imprisonable flag abuse?

As for the flag itself, would this proposed amendment permit incarceration were someone to manufacture paper towels with an American flag motif? Could you play football on a muddy field wearing a Tommy Hilfiger shirt with a flag across the chest? Could you eat an ice cream cake flag? What might happen to someone who disrespects a picture of a flag, or an actual flag with 48 or 52 stars? While criminal defense attorneys may prosper, the proposed amendment would create a nightmare for prosecutors and judges, and could be used for unintended censorship.

Answer to Ignorant, Repugnant Speech: More Speech, Not Less

In its opinion in the Johnson case, the Supreme Court stated: "We can imagine no more appropriate response to burning a flag than by waving one's own. . . The way to preserve the flag's special role is not to punish those who feel differently about these matters. It is to persuade them that they are wrong." In 1976, a crowd at Wrigley Field in Chicago actually burst into a spontaneous rendition of "God Bless America" when two protesters ran onto the field and tried to burn a flag. How utterly, beautifully American a response!

Arresting someone who is demonstrating peacefully, if utterly obnoxiously, only vindicates that person's hatred. Legislation cannot change the hearts and minds of men nearly so effectively as education. As to false or repugnant speech, Supreme Court Justice Louis Frankfurter once wrote: "[T]he remedy to be applied is more speech, not enforced silence."

Conclusion

The proposed amendment not only would be ineffective at accomplishing its stated purpose of protecting the flag from desecration; it would itself desecrate the Constitution and the Bill of Rights. Americans who believe that desecration of the American flag must be outlawed are allowing an emotional reaction to something they find highly offensive overrule the well-reasoned conclusions of our Founding Fathers.

Protecting the Flag Is Patriotism, Not Censorship

Patrick Brady

The following selection is an excerpt from a speech by Patrick Brady to an audience at The American Legion Eighty-third Annual National Convention in 2001. Brady is a retired major general of the U.S. Army and chairman of the board of the Citizens Flag Alliance, a coalition against any desecration of the American flag. He praises the American Legion's support for legislation proposed to add an amendment to the U.S. Constitution that would outlaw desecration of the flag. Brady writes that most Americans find flag desecration to be offensive and evil, and that the majority should be able to dictate limitations to offensive conduct. The flag represents the Constitution, and therefore any act that harms the flag also desecrates the Constitution. Brady states that developing respect for the flag is a mandatory lesson in patriotism that Americans must pass on to their children in order to preserve freedom.

Your [Members of the American Legion,] legacy encompasses monumental accomplishments. The GI Bill which enabled the greatest generation to build the greatest nation in history. Today the youth you developed continue the tradition of patriotism and represent all that is good in America at every level of service and leadership. But what you are doing for our Constitution through the flag Amendment may be your greatest legacy.

Arguments Against a Flag Amendment

The enemy today is more formidable than any you faced on the battlefield. The debate in the House on the flag high-

Patrick Brady, "Message Points on Flag Protection," www.cfa-inc.org, August 28, 2001. Reproduced by permission.

lighted the great divide in our nation on the Constitution and the very definition of patriotism. Our opposition defines the essence of freedom as the toleration of unpatriotic conduct.

They actually separate our freedoms from patriotism and have their own version of patriotism. And they separate our laws from our values. They say the flag symbolizes the freedom to burn it; that our flag is the symbol of un-patriotic conduct. That burning the symbol of patriotism is patriotic.

They cower before the courts, they believe the courts not "WE THE PEOPLE" rule. And for good reason. Many of them know that their agenda could never survive in the bright lights of the public square, where the people rule. Their only hope is in the courtroom where the dark robed un-elected elite rule.

In the hostility of the media environment in which we all live, sound bites are the norm. It is true that if one can control the language, control of minds is not far behind. In a few seconds opinion is formed and laws are made. Tragically, many sound bits are false and misleading and we are led astray.

American Values Honor Protecting the Flag

For this reason it is vital that we fill our quiver with truth bites as we go into battle with those who would disfigure America and teach our children flag desecration is speech. We must out communicate them. We cannot repeat too often these truths.

Never forget that the foundation of all we are doing for the flag is the Constitution. The Constitution is the foundation of all we are and the only guarantee of our future. It is under attack and little understood by too many of our people.

To those who say that burning the flag is speech, ask what is said when the flag is burned. Ask how you burn a flag with your tongue. Tommy Lasorda said that speech is when you talk. Our opponents believe they are wiser than 80% of the people, 70% of the Congress, 4 Chief Justices of the United

States as well as Justices on 5 other Supreme Courts in the last century who agree with Tommy.

If they disagree with this mighty armada of flag defenders ask them if they also disagree with James Madison, who wrote the first amendment, and Thomas Jefferson who also agree with Tommy. [Congressman] Richard Gephardt, MO, was right in condemning those who seek to distort our Constitution while cloaking themselves in a disguise of free speech.

The Flag *Is* the Constitution

To those who say the flag is precious to them but the Constitution is more precious, ask if they have any possession that is precious to them, any one or anything that they love, that they would not protect. Pat Boone compared this to saying that he loved his mother but it was okay to bat her around.

If they say they do not want to amend the Constitution for the flag tell them that we are not amending the Constitution for the flag, we are doing it for the Constitution.

To those who worry about making felons of flag burners, tell them we oppose that. Tell them that flag burners are not the problem; the problem is those who distort our Constitution by calling flag burning speech.

To all who find virtue in bashing our values, who say we must tolerate conduct that the majority find offensive or evil, ask where that is written in the Constitution.

If anyone says this amendment damages the constitution, read the amendment to them and remind them that it damages nothing because it changes nothing; it simply restores the Constitution to its original meaning, the meaning of the founders.

If they say flag protection aligns us with dictatorships, ask them how a flag protected according to the will of a free people, a flag designed by the Father of our country, could be compared to a flag protected according to the will of a tyrant.

Madison and Jefferson believed our flag should be protected, does that align them with Hitler and Stalin?

Ask them if they have ever heard of the prisoners of war of a dictatorship fashioning bits of cloth or toilet paper into a swastika or a hammer and sickle. Ask them if any [prisoners of war (POWs)] ever have ever said a pledge to the flag of a dictator. Tell them that Americans have done this for Old Glory in every war.

If they say flag burning does not happen often, tell them once is to often.

Ask them what frequency has to do with what is right and wrong.

More Problems with the Opposition's Claims

To those who say the Supreme Court is the final word, tell them that in our Constitution, the people are the final word. Ask them how the Supreme Court could rule that flag burning is speech, and allow it to be burned anywhere—but on their steps.

If they quote Colin Powell that the flag amendment is not worth it to hammer a few miscreants, tell them our goal is not to hammer miscreants, our goal is to hammer the Supreme Court, they are the miscreants in this case. Remind them that General Schwartzkopf said he considered the protection of our flag an absolute necessity, and a matter of critical importance to our nation.

Tell them that President [George W.] Bush said he strongly supported the flag amendment because of, among other things, a debt to your legacy of sacrifice and service.

If they say they want to protect the flag but only by statute, tell them that the flag amendment will require a statute for protection, in fact it is the only way to get a statute.

Ask your representatives if they are for hate crime legislation. Then ask if burning the flag is a hate crime.

If they are confused with the difference between the Legion burning a worn out flag and some one burning or defecating on a new flag, explain the word desecrate to them. It is not a flag burning amendment it is a flag desecration amendment.

If they tell you we cannot legislate patriotism, tell them that patriotism is the last refuge of a free people and that every law we pass should inspire, should teach, should endorse, and should ensure patriotism in the people. Patriotism is simply love of country; our land, our neighbors, and our leaders. The first duty of every citizen is to be patriots and to make patriots of our children.

The notion that irresponsible, disrespectful conduct is necessary for freedom is not new but it is nonsense, not to be found anywhere in our Constitution. To separate freedom from patriotism is tragic. Patriots are the very source, often the fodder, of freedom. There is no freedom without patriots.

If they say the flag amendment reflects a tyranny of the majority, an effort to force their will on a more "virtuous" minority, ask them then if the minority of the Supreme Court, who wanted the flag protected, was more virtuous than the majority who said flag burning is speech. And ask them if the minority who would have elected their opponent, was more virtuous than the majority that elected them.

If they say we are trying to amend the Bill of Rights for the first time, ask if the Supreme Court had voted to protect the flag, would they then have amended the Bill of Rights.

If they were among those in the last election who said that every vote must count, or who during the impeachment process said we must listen to the people, remind them that is exactly what we are asking, listen to the people, let every voice count.

If they have trouble defining the American flag and feign concern about prosecuting those who burn bikinis embroidered with the flag or toilet paper marked with the flag, ask them if they would put toilet paper or a bikini on the flag of a veteran, or raise them from a flag pole during retreat.

If anyone says the flag represents the freedom to burn it, that our military died on the battlefields of the world so their flag could be burned on the street corners of America, warn them not to say that to a veteran.

Protection of the Flag Must Be Vigilant

Our struggle is made more difficult because it seems not to be measurable in material terms. To find champions with the moral courage to fight for a cause without material benefit can be difficult.

It frequently seems there are precious few who will do something simply because it is the right thing to do. Many shake their heads in disbelief that we would work so hard for something that promised no monetary benefit to any one, and has in fact cost much in time and treasure for those involved.

The truth is that all the prosperity and material wealth we enjoy is the result of the sacrifices of many who gave all they had simply because it was the right thing to do. Their sacrifices certainly were not materially measurable to them but have been immeasurable to America. Our children need to know this.

To ensure that the outrageous conduct of a minority does not outweigh the will of the majority goes counter to will of the elite, but it is the right thing to do.

To begin restoring the true meaning of the First Amendment, and remind the Courts that the people own the Constitution, doesn't make us a dime, but it does help stop those who would remake our Constitution. And it is the right thing to do. To return to our children a protected priceless teaching aid for patriotism won't make us rich, but it will enrich their lives. And it is the right thing to do. To remind politicians that our laws should reflect our values has no price tag, but the results can be priceless. And it is the right thing to do. Our bottom line is not the dollar bill, it is the Bill of Rights, it is the right of the people to define the meaning of their Constitution, and that is the right thing to do.

For those who question our efforts, our question to them is—how do you stop doing what is right?

I recall with pride a conversation between a flag skeptic and an American Legion official. The skeptic expressed alarm over how much had been spent on the Flag Amendment and asked how much more we would spend. He was told we would spend whatever it took. Why? Simply because it is the right thing to do.

Once again you are engaged in a great battle. Once again you are standing for what is right. Today you do not stand against tanks and rockets and missiles. Your wounds will not be mortal. But the wounds to America could be if your kind of patriotism dies. It is my great honor to stand with you.

The Controversy over Internet Filters in Libraries

The Why Files

In the twenty-first century the majority of American youth use the Internet regularly for personal enjoyment and homework. This explosion in Internet usage has generated considerable debate about the moral considerations related to online access for children and teenagers. Since pornography and violent content are accessible with only a click of the mouse, many concerned parents and educators have called for libraries to use of Internet filters that block objectionable content while young people surf the World Wide Web. Other parents, teachers, and librarians have expressed reservations about filters on the grounds that they censor material in a public forum and thus compromise the First Amendment rights of Internet users. In this selection the authors of the Why Files website explains the Internet filter controversy in the context of the Children's Internet Protection Act (CIPA) legislation that was upheld by the U.S. Supreme Court in 1993. CIPA requires schools and libraries that receive federal funding to protect minors from viewing child pornography and obscene visual depictions while using computers with online access. The article explains how internet filtering programs work, describes common problems with using filters to enforce CIPA, and outlines the debate about whether protecting children from Internet obscenity unduly imposes on their civil liberties. The Why Files Web site, based at the University of Wisconsin-Madison, is dedicated to explaining contemporary issues in science, math, and technology in a clear, accessible, and accurate manner for the public.

The Why Files, "Access Denied: Fighting Filth or Filtering the First Amendment?" http://whyfiles.org, July 2003. Reproduced by permission.

L ast month, [June 2003] the U.S. Supreme Court upheld the Children's Internet Protection Act, or CIPA. If public libraries don't filter access to the Internet, they will lose federal funding for computers and Internet connections. Depending on your perspective, the decision represents a victory for morality, or a disaster for the first amendment, which says, "Congress shall make no law respecting an establishment of religion, or prohibiting the free exercise thereof; *or abridging the freedom of speech, or of the press*; or the right of the people peaceably to assemble, and to petition the government for a redress of grievances."

CIPA was passed in 2000 after the court deep-sixed two previous attempts to regulate Internet porn. . . . The newly upheld law essentially requires that public schools and libraries install blocking software on all computers accessible to the public—whether or not they will be used by children under age 16—the wards that CIPA has taken under its wing.

Surfing in Schools and Libraries

The filtering dispute exists against a background of exploding use of the Internet by young people: In 2001, almost 60 percent of kids aged 5 to 17 used the Internet, according to researcher Paul Resnick of the University of Michigan. By 2002, 76.9 percent of U.S. schools were using filters, according to Quality Education Data's Internet Usage in Teaching 2002 report.

These statistics, and the glut of porn sites available at the click of a mouse, have fostered the federal interest in preventing kids trom viewing porn.

In schools and libraries, Internet blocking (or "filtering") software generally operates through the server or network, not in the individual computer. When the user requests a website, the software checks a list of banned sites, then displays the page or blocks it—sometimes without any notice to the user.

Even though both the humans and the electronic robots that maintain the blocking lists are prone to error, the court held that CIPA safeguarded the first-amendment rights of library users because anyone 16 or older could simply ask a librarian to shut off the filters.

Problems with the "Shut-Off" System

The "shut-it-off" solution may sound benign, but making that request could be embarrassing, says Kristin Eschenfelder, an assistant professor in the University of Wisconsin-Madison School of Library and Information Studies. "Imagine you're a 16-year-old kid in Provo, Utah, and you think you are gay, and your mom and dad know the librarians. Are you going to be comfortable asking for [the filter] to be turned off?" The victims of the new law, she says, "will be at the fringe, people who are already at risk in certain areas. . . the oddballs from all ends of the spectrum. Everybody has a right to use the library, but will it get back to your family that you asked for the filter to be turned off?"

The court decision alarmed many librarians, who denounced it as censorship, an infringement on the free speech that is a core value for a profession that celebrates "banned books week."

Some problems start with the definition used in the law. CIPA specifies that library computers not deliver content that would be graphically obscene or "harmful to minors." Librarians insist that both standards are elusive. "Harmful to minors" is vague. And only human beings can interpret whether a graphic file is obscene.

"Any analyses that have been done pretty clearly show that the companies are not following the legal definition about what is 'harmful to minors' or obscene," says Jane Pearlmutter, associate director of the School of Library and Information Studies at UW-Madison, "so the decisions are not being made in any consistent way."

At any rate, the problem that CIPA is meant to solve is overstated, says Pearlmutter, who provides continuing education to librarians around the United States. "I've heard very few librarians saying that it's a big problem, that people are there mainly to search for porn."

Problems with Filters

Yet as public libraries confront a legal requirement to choose a filter or forego money, they cannot determine just how the filters operate, Pearlmutter says. "The reason the ALA [American Library Association] has been so active on this issue is because the filters block so much, and they have called over and over for discussion of what sites are being blocked, who is deciding, and what criteria are being used and that is never forthcoming [from the filtering companies]".

The ALA held that "the use of filtering software by libraries to block access to constitutionally protected speech violates the Library Bill of Rights. Note in particular paragraph III: "Libraries should challenge censorship in the fulfillment of their responsibility to provide information and enlightenment."

Finally, on a practical note, critics charge, blocking software both under-filters—allows smut to reach the screen—and over-filters—blocks non-pornographic stuff. You can see over-filtering in action from this test of Internet filters by Harvard law student Ben Edelman. In 2001, while preparing evidence for an American Civil Liberties Union challenge to CIPA, Edelman found that if you:

- Need coping hints after an amputation, you'd have been out of luck if your public library computer was hobbled by the N2H2 filter, which cut off the site as "Adults Only, Pornography"

- Want to help stray animals in Los Angeles, you'd have been impounded for surfing to this site—from a computer leashed by Cyberpatrol or reined in by Websense.

- Need to translate English into Urdu? This English-Urdu dictionary was unavailable from a Cyberpatrolled computer, which defined that titillating tome as "Adult/Sexually Explicit."

- Don't try cooking up homebrew if you use Smartfilter, which blended the site into its "Mature" category.

- Religion may be the opiate of the masses, but Websense injected the Agape church into its "Adult Content" wastebasket. . . .

How Do Filters Work?

Disappointingly, the nuts-and-bolts of web filters remains an area of darkness. We do know that many filtering systems start by putting websites into categories—such as adult, gambling, or illegal MP3 downloads. The system administrator or computer owner then decides which categories are permissible.

Some filters also employ a keyword filter that is triggered by words or phrases like "breast," "porn," "sex," or "hot girls." Keyword-blocking has been criticized for blocking access to sites related to, say, "breast cancer" or "sexual health," but it's the kind of data-intensive activity that can easily be computerized, and is certainly cheap. . . .

Often, an entire domain, like all of nasa.gov or whitehouse.gov is blocked if any page within it is adjudged objectionable.

In categorizing websites, filter makers generally claim to use a combination of digital and human scanning. They will not, however, reveal exactly what standards they use, or what sites they block. "There is no way to get the block list, you can't go to Google, for example, and ask them, say tell me everything," says Edelman. "Similarly, with the commercial services, they are not interested in telling you." Indeed, he argues that "the categorization scheme is absolutely a black box, you don't know the professional qualifications of the content classification staff, and those qualifications are dubious, given the mind-numbing work they have to do day in and day out."

The Why Files tried to ask Websense, a major vendor of software to libraries, about its procedures, but they did not return our phone calls. Some blocking vendors do allow you to check if a particular URL is blocked, but as critics point out, the blocking lists can change daily, so it can be difficult to know about, let alone comply with, the decisions of the many vendors in the business.

It's easy to understand why firms would want to conceal trade secrets, but the lack of information puts librarians and operators of web sites at a disadvantage. Will the software block legitimate searches related to health? Could The Why Files be blocked because we discuss, say, web filters that restrict porn?

Filtering the Filth

While concerned parents worry that the Internet will give their kids access to a degrading world of depraved sexuality, many librarians worry about civil liberties. The fact that paid defenders of the first amendment run many libraries explains why some big-city districts, including Chicago and Los Angeles, may forego federal funds and forget filters.

Other library officials are waiting for details about costs. Barbara Dimick, director of the Madison (Wis.) Public Library, says her system is waiting to learn how much federal money will be affected by the ruling, but she's been unimpressed by filters to date. "We did a search two to three years ago, and the filters were remarkably awful, tended to screen out what you wanted to research, and not take care of all the sites that might be considered objectionable."

But while some large library systems may forego federal support in favor of setting their own Internet policies, others have taken a different tack. For one thing, for all that lip service about free speech, viewing pornography is a real problem in some public libraries. "I have talked to a couple of students from big urban libraries who say it's very stressful," says Kristin Eschenfelder of the UW-Madison. "If a patron with a substance abuse problem or who is not totally mentally there comes in, using a workstation . . . this person might be really scary, or threaten you when you tell him you can't use a computer." Some libraries that don't restrict porn on computers are facing sexual harassment lawsuits from their employees, who are disgusted by repeatedly clearing porn from computer screens.

More important, filters may be better than critics say. Hampton (Skip) Auld, assistant director of Chesterfield County Public Library, near Richmond, Va., has publicly argued that the filters work. For two years, he says, his library has heeded a local decision to restrict Internet use, and, "There has been minimal over-and underblocking of sites." During those two years, in a system that serves 1.5 million visitors annually, he says, librarians have logged about 40 requests to unblock, and 39 to add blocks. "I have a high level of confidence that filters can be configured in a way that will minimize the over-underblocking problem," Auld says.

Critics, we must point out, counter that library users aren't always asking to have filters lifted. "I'm not sure the librarians are in any particular position to say," says Edelman. "They only know if a patron comes up and complains, and you have to be an awfully confident patron to know you have been overblocked . . . and complain. We are all trained to defer to the computer, if it tells you you are asking for a porn site, and you can't have it, that's an embarrassing thing."

Controlling the Filters

Still, Auld says a key to success is setting the filter accurately. Instead of filtering broadly, Chesterfield chose "minimal categories, only those that are meant to deal with obscenity, child pornography, or 'harmful to minors material.'" With only two of the five "adult categories" blocked, users should be able to reach sex education, swimsuit and lingerie sites. The block-by-word feature, long a bugaboo of filter opponents, is off.

Filters are working, Auld insists. When the county surveyed librarians, the number who said they had to clear porn from screens daily plummeted.

As a librarian who says filters can work, Auld admits he's become a pariah "in some circles," but says, "I've tried to speak from experience . . . I'm not saying everybody should use the filters. I don't think CIPA was a good law, mainly because these things should be worked out locally. I don't think filters are necessary in all situations. I'm saying that the filters work better than they have been made out to work."

A Matter of Degree

Behind the black-and-white dispute over filters lurks an interesting question of selectivity. Most filters can be configured to be more or less restrictive, and those settings really matter, says Paul Resnick, an associate professor of information sciences at the University of Michigan. Last December, Resnick and a colleague published a report on the filtering of health information sites, and found that configurations had a massive effect on the results.

Websites were chosen for the test if they "had any information that would be discussed in a school of medicine or a school of public health," Resnick explained. When the researchers set six filters at minimum restriction, and tried to reach the sites, an average of 1.3 percent were blocked.

That low number hides the fact that some topics faced much greater censorship. Even at the least restrictive setting, Resnick says, ". . . about 10 percent of the controversial sites were blocked," including sites related to condoms, safe sex and gay health. At an intermediate setting, he says, 20 percent of gay-related sites were blocked.

Those results highlight a need to recognize shades of grey in the Internet filtering debate, Resnick says. "The debate has been black-and-white—do we want the filters or not—but I think we have to get beyond that and discuss what sort of overrides we want, and how we choose the settings."

Where Does this Leave Libraries?

For better or worse, filters are becoming another expense for libraries, which must either buy software (about $10 to $20 per computer per year at the Chesterfield County libraries) or forego federal money and find another way to control inappropriate use of the Internet.

Linda Mielke, a former President of the Public Library Association, a division of the American Library Association, says it's time to accept filters and move on. Mielke, who directs the Carroll County (Maryland) Public Library, explains her reasoning: "Say I didn't filter, what am I going to argue? I could say the Supreme Court is wrong; I don't think so. I could say it violates the first amendment; it didn't. I could say I don't need the money, but I'm not willing as a custodian of the public library to make any of those arguments—I'm thinking of the long-term health of the public library system I run."

Key to convincing the court, she says, was the argument that adults who dislike filters can ask a librarian to shut them off. And while many librarians argue that this is difficult or impossible on short notice, because a computer technician might be needed, Mielke insists that with the N2H2 filter at her library, it "takes 5 seconds. . . . If you go to a blocked site, and that's pretty hard to do, you ask the librarian to unblock it for you."

On the other hand, however, nobody seems ecstatic with the Court decision, at least according to Robed Drechsel, who follows first-amendment issues at the School of Journalism and Mass Communication at the University of Wisconsin-Madison. "Everybody seems to acknowledge, even the justices who voted for the decision, that filtering is imperfect, that there is a real risk of over-filtering or under-filtering," he says. "That's the somewhat frustrating thing, the court essentially approved a remedy that it simultaneously admits could sweep too broadly and too narrowly."

Librarians Organize to Fight Censorship

Tom Teepen

The Freedom to Read Foundation (FTRF) was founded in 1969 to help libraries provide the general public unobstructed access to books and other information. In this selection, writer Tom Teepen explains how the American Library Association (ALA) saw a need for a separate but associated organization to fight First Amendment battles in court, thus giving librarians the support to defend freedom of speech in their communities. Teepan writes that such nongovernmental organizations have been essential to protecting freedom of speech in the United States—by monitoring cases of censorship, providing legal expertise to those being censored, and vigilantly challenging censorship attempts. The FTRF has joined with the ALA to fight against the banning of books, Congressional attempts to impose filters on library Internet access, and library regulations required by the USA Patriot Act. Teepen is a columnist for Cox Newspapers and served on the FTRF Board of Trustees from 2003 to 2005.

Reporting On His Own 1735 Trial for seditious libel for his disrespect of the Crown, colonial printer and *New York Weekly Journal* Editor John Peter Zenger wrote that when the jury brought in a verdict of not guilty "there were three huzzahs in the hall." Americans who prize their press and speech freedoms have been cheering ever since. Zenger's release, after 10 months in jail for publishing articles critical of New York Colonial Governor William Cosby, was a milestone on the way to the Bill of Rights, with its First Amendment admonition that "Congress shall make no law . . . abridging the freedom of speech, or of the press."

These 14 words were a second American revolution in their own right, indeed a revolution in human affairs, though one still sadly incomplete in most of the world. For all that the principle is embraced in the United Nation's Universal Declaration of Human Rights, the rights to free speech and a free press remain far from universal. Few nations even approach the breadth of protected expression that is secured by the U.S. Constitution's First Amendment.

The Freedom to Read

Even here, our own freedoms to publish, distribute, and openly debate information and opinion remain under stress. Free speech is perhaps the purest example of the liberty whose price is "eternal vigilance," abolitionist Wendell Phillips said.

That vigilance is maintained in large part by a number of organizations committed to the free speech that too many Americans—often in positions of political power—would honor in principle while undermining it in practice. Among those defenders, count the American Civil Liberties Union, the American Booksellers Foundation for Free Expression, the Association of American Publishers, and the Freedom to Read Foundation (FTRF). Established in 1969 by the American Library Association, the FTRF was formed in recognition of the fact that a robust defense of the First Amendment is fundamental to the very essence of libraries as the crucial nexus that offers unimpeded access to society's wisdom, wit, folly, and frolic in all their confounding and sometimes cussed variety.

An offshoot of ALA's Office for Intellectual Freedom (OIF), the FTRF has been in court more or less constantly throughout its 35-year history and currently has more than a dozen active cases. The FTRF concentrates on issues that impact librarians and library' practices but additionally joins with other First Amendment defenders in broader free-speech cases.

The foundation recognizes that any chipping away at the First Amendment weakens it.

In its first year, the FTRF helped to defend a librarian who had been fired from the Missouri State Library for writing a letter to a local newspaper protesting the suppression of an underground newspaper. It helped a Maryland man challenge his conviction for selling an allegedly obscene issue of the *Washington Free Press*; a state appellate court overturned the conviction. And the foundation helped defray the financial hit that the city librarian of Martinsville Virginia, had taken after coming under fire for challenging the constitutionality of a religious course taught in the city schools.

Supporting Librarians

ALA's OIF set up shop in 1967 to chart censorship trends and alert librarians to them, as well as to provide resource materials to local libraries that found items in their collections being challenged. The office could back up local librarians with national reviews of besieged books and suggest effective talking points. With ready access to such reinforcement, local librarians were both more willing and better able to defend the content of their shelves. Judith Krug, director of OIF from its beginning, says, "When people began to realize they had support here, they began to develop backbones." Before then, Krug says, local librarians who tried to resist pressure to reject or remove books were "the lone voice in the wilderness."

Understandably, many shied away from that role. But as helpful as all that support was, and remains, Krug and others quickly realized that libraries also needed access to ready, committed, and expert legal support. As much as they needed advocacy in the political and social arenas, they need a champion in the legal lists, too.

The FTRF was created as the First Amendment legal arm of ALA, not formally attached to the association, but connected: Four ALA officers hold interlocking memberships on the 15-member FTRF board. Ten members are elected by an annual mail ballot of FTRF members, many of whom also belong to ALA. Krug, also a board member, wears a second hat as the foundation's executive director, and for years served as its only staff member. There is now one other full-time staffer, and some ALA staff do double duty working for the foundation.

An early and key decision by the FTRF board based the foundation revenues primarily on membership funding, rather than on contributions from large private or corporate donors, helping to insulate the FTRF from the pressures major givers sometimes try to apply and keeping it free of the strings some might want to attach. The membership, drawn mainly from ALA's ranks, hovers around 1,800. The basic dues are $35 annually.

At first, ALA counsel represented the foundation, but as the FTRF caseload increased in both number and complexity, it became clear that the FTRF needed its own attorney. It has been represented by the Washington, D.C. office of Jenner and Block, a firm that specializes in First Amendment law.

Key Court Battles

Sometimes the FTRF files legal challenges directly, especially when the core mission of libraries is at risk. For instance, it joined with ALA in 1996 to contest the Communications Decency Act, a law that, like many before and since, used a declared concern for children as a means to attempt much broader suppression of materials some might consider risqué. In 2001, the foundation once again joined ALA in a lawsuit challenging the Children's Internet Protection Act—a law requiring libraries receiving federal funds to defray telecommunication expenses to install filters on their internet computers. Although the Supreme Court ultimately upheld CIPA as a legitimate condition of funding, the justices made it clear that adults could not be blocked from accessing constitutionally protected material on the interact by emphasizing that libraries must disable filters at the request of adult users.

The foundation has, of course, soldiered through many wars over denounced books—from Kurt Vonnegut's *Slaughterhouse-Five* (Delacorte, 1969) through Eldrige Cleaver's *Soul on Ice* (McGraw-Hill, 1967) and the anonymously penned *Go Ask Alice* (Prentice-Hall, 1971) to Michael Willhoite's *Daddy's Roommate* (Alyson Wonderland, 1990) and Lesléa Newman's *Heather Has Two Mommies* (Alyson Wonderland, 2000) and such classics as *Lysistrata* by Aristophanes and Geoffrey Chaucer's *The Miller's Tale*.

It is through amicus briefs that the foundation most often appears in court. These friend-of-the-court filings broaden and add weight to ongoing First Amendment claims against a variety of legislation and local policies that would restrict access to published material.

With the singular "press" of Zenger's *New York Weekly Journal* having long since proliferated into the plural "media," First Amendment issues have multiplied and become increasingly complex. Recent years have found the FTRF particularly busy opposing harmful-to-minors and child-protection legislation that sponsors use as a backdoor method to restrict material, including even scientific reports, that is intended for adults. Consistent victories in federal courts have not stopped Congress from passing virtually the same legislation over and over again, with the wording tweaked a little this way or that. And state legislatures frequently mimic even those federal statutes that already have been declared unconstitutional, requiring still more litigation.

National Challenges

While much of the foundation's legal work involves it in cases bearing broad, national implications, the FTRF also jumps into community challenges. In 1999, the foundation helped the library in Wichita Falls, Texas, prepare a successful legal challenge to a city ordinance requiring it to move titles from its children's area to the adult section if 300 people signed a petition requesting it. Library circulations of videotapes and CDs have brought new challenges, adding struggles over images to the traditional tug-of-war over words. Internet issues are now so numerous that they are becoming a body of case law in their own right. And globalization is producing new and increasingly worrisome threats. An FTRF amicus brief supported Yahoo! against a French court's findings that the internet provider was liable for hosting customer pages on its United States site advertising Nazi and racist memorabilia that are illegal in France.

The USA Patriot Act, hastily drawn and enacted in reaction to 9/11 terrorism, has created a bewildering new array of First Amendment jeopardies. In coordination with other civil liberties organizations, the FTRF is in the thick of the legal fights over the act's extraordinary reach. The Patriot Act's infamous Section 215, for instance, expands the FBI's authority to demand library records and requires library workers to keep such intrusions secret.

The FTRF has argued that both the gag order and the act's failure to require any showing of relevance to a terrorist threat violated the constitutional right to freely transmit and receive information. The FTRF also supported an ACLU challenge to the Patriot Act's Section 505 provisions allowing the FBI to issue national security letters without judicial oversight, arguing that it threatens the rights of libraries, bookstores, and their patrons as well as internet communications in general.

Andrew Hamilton, John Peter Zenger's attorney, praised the jury that vindicated the printer in 1735, declaring that the verdict had "baffled the attempt of tyranny" and had "given us a right to liberty of both exposing and opposing arbitrary power . . . by speaking and writing truth." The FTRF's filings add to the growing body of First Amendment precedents upholding that tradition. They are often cited in court rulings and are so respected that, at one point, a New York judge held off making a decision until he could consult the foundation's views.

"We bring to this area," Krug said, "a reputation that we do a societal good."

Feminists Against Pornography

Susan Brownmiller

Susan Brownmiller is best known for writing Against Our Will: Men, Women, and Rape *in 1975. The book was a pioneering analysis of the politics of rape from the perspective of a radical feminist during the women's liberation movement of the early 1970s. The following selection was written in 1979 when Brownmiller and other New York radical feminists founded Women Against Pornography, an activist organization protesting the public display of pornography that degraded women. In her essay, Brownmiller is careful to acknowledge the importance of freedom of speech in America. Unlike many who oppose pornography, Brownmiller does not condemn erotic art or expressions of sexual desire. Her objection to pornography focuses on the way the often violent images in popular pornographic magazines and movies degrade and dehumanize the female body. Rather than advocating outright censorship of pornography, she demands that it not be displayed openly. Such commonplace public display of degrading images, she argues, forces women to view pornography against their will, causing them considerable harm.*

Brownmiller is currently a professor of Women's and Gender Studies at Pace University in New York City.

Free speech is one of the great foundations on which our democracy rests. I am old enough to remember the Hollywood Ten, the screenwriters who went to jail in the late 1940's because they refused to testify before a congressional committee about their political affiliations. They tried to use the First Amendment as a defense, but they went to jail because in those days there were few civil liberties lawyers around who

Susan Brownmiller, "Let's Put Pornography Back in the Closet," *Newsday*, 1979. Reproduced by permission of the author.

cared to champion the First Amendment right to free speech, when the speech concerned the Communist Party.

The Hollywood Ten were correct in claiming the First Amendment. Its high purpose is the protection of unpopular ideas and political dissent. In the dark, cold days of the 1950's, few civil libertarians were willing to declare themselves First Amendment absolutists. But in the brighter, though frantic, days of the 1960's, the principle of protecting unpopular political speech was gradually strengthened.

It is fair to say now that the battle has largely been won. Even the American Nazi Party has found itself the beneficiary of the dedicated, tireless work of the American Civil Liberties Union. But—and please notice the quotation marks coming up—"To equate the free and robust exchange of ideas and political debate with commercial exploitation of obscene material demeans the grand conception of the First Amendment and its high purposes in the historic struggle for freedom. It is a misuse of the great guarantees of free speech and free press."

I didn't say that, although I wish I had, for I think the words are thrilling. Chief Justice Warren Burger said it in 1973, in the United States Supreme Court's majority opinion in *Miller v. California*. During the same decades that the right to political free speech was being strengthened in the courts, the nation's obscenity laws also were undergoing extensive revision.

Important Victories for Free Speech

It's amazing to recall that in 1934 the question of whether James Joyce's *Ulysses* should be banned as pornographic actually went before the Court. The battle to protect *Ulysses* as a work of literature with redeeming social value was won. In later decades, Henry Miller's Tropic books, *Lady Chatterley's Lover* and the *Memoirs of Fanny Hill* also were adjudged not obscene. These decisions have been important to me. As the author of *Against Our Will*, a study of the history of rape that does contain explicit sexual material, I shudder to think how my book would have fared if James Joyce, D. H. Lawrence and Henry Miller hadn't gone before me.

I am not a fan of *Chatterley* or the Tropic books, I should quickly mention. They are not to my literary taste, nor do I think they represent female sexuality with any degree of accuracy. But I would hardly suggest that we ban them. Such a suggestion wouldn't get very far anyway. The battle to protect these books is ancient history. Time does march on, quite methodically. What, then, is unlawfully obscene, and what does the First Amendment have to do with it?

Defining "Obscene"

In the Miller case of 1973 (not Henry Miller, by the way, but a porn distributor who sent unsolicited stuff through the mails), the Court came up with new guidelines that it hoped would strengthen obscenity laws by giving more power to the states. What it did in actuality was throw everything into confusion. It set up a three-part test by which materials can be adjudged obscene. The materials are obscene if they depict patently offensive, hardcore sexual conduct; lack serious scientific, literary, artistic or political value, and appeal to the prurient interest of an average personas measured by contemporary community standards.

"Patently offensive," "prurient interest" and "hardcore" are indeed words to conjure with. "Contemporary community standards" are what we're trying to redefine. The feminist objection to pornography is not based on prurience, which the dictionary defines as lustful, itching desire. We are not opposed to sex and desire, with or without the itch, and we certainly believe that explicit sexual material has its place in literature, art, science and education. Here we part company rather swiftly with oldline conservatives who don't want sex education in the high schools, for example.

No, the feminist objection to pornography is based on our belief that pornography represents hatred of women, that pornography's intent is to humiliate, degrade and dehumanize the female body for the purpose of erotic stimulation and pleasure. We are unalterably opposed to the presentation of the female body being stripped, bound, raped, tortured, mutilated and murdered in the name of commercial entertainment and free speech.

Slick Sadism

These images, which are standard pornographic fare, have nothing to do with the hallowed right of political dissent. They have everything to do with the creation of a cultural climate in which a rapist feels he is merely giving in to a normal urge and a woman is encouraged to believe that sexual masochism is healthy, liberated fun. Justice Potter Stewart once said about hardcore pornography, "You know it when you see it," and that certainly used to be true. In the good old days, pornography looked awful. It was cheap and sleazy, and there was no mistaking it for art.

Nowadays, since the porn industry has become a multi-million dollar business, visual technology has been employed in its service. Pornographic movies are skillfully filmed and edited, pornographic still shots using the newest tenets of good design artfully grace the covers of *Hustler, Penthouse*, and *Playboy*, and the public and the courts are sadly confused.

The Supreme Court neglected to define "hardcore" in the Miller decision. This was a mistake. If "hardcore" refers only to explicit sexual intercourse, then that isn't good enough. When women or children or men, no matter how artfully, are shown tortured or terrorized in the service of sex, that's obscene. And "patently offensive," I would hope, to our "contemporary community standards."

Put Porn Out of Sight

Justice William O. Douglas wrote in his dissent to the Miller case that no one is "compelled to look." This is hardly true. To buy a paper at the corner newsstand is to subject oneself to a forcible immersion in pornography, to be demeaned by an array of dehumanized, chopped up parts of the female anatomy, packaged like cuts of meat at the supermarket. I happen to like my body and I work hard at the gym to keep it in good shape, but I am embarrassed for my body and for the bodies of all women when I see the fragmented parts of us so frivolously, and so flagrantly, displayed.

Some constitutional theorists (Justice Douglas was one) have maintained that any obscenity law is a serious abridgment of free speech. Others (and Justice Earl Warren was one) have maintained that the First Amendment was never intended to protect obscenity. We live quite compatibly with a host of free speech abridgements. There are restraints against false and misleading advertising or statements shouting "fire" without cause in a crowded movie theater, etc. that do not threaten, but strengthen, our societal values. Restrictions on the public display of pornography belong in this category.

The distinction between permission to publish and permission to display publicly is an essential one and one which I think consonant with First Amendment principles. Justice Burger's words which I quoted above support this without question. We are not saying "Smash the presses" or "Ban the bad ones," but simply "Get the stuff out of our sight." Let the legislatures decide—using realistic and humane contemporary community standards—what can be displayed and what cannot. The courts, after all, will be the final arbiters.

Censorship of Popular Music in Contemporary America

Paul D. Fischer

Historian Paul D. Fischer is a professor in the department of re-
cording industry at Middle Tennessee State University in Mur-
freesboro, Tennessee. In the following selection he outlines the
major controversies over the censorship of contemporary popular
music in America. He describes various civil and criminal court
cases that have focused on whether certain music is obscene, con-
tains "inciteful speech" leading to violence, or is harmful to mi-
nors. He also notes that to date, America's courts have blocked
most of the efforts by legislators to censor the content of popular
music. However, in 1985 the Recording Industry Association of
America did implement a voluntary Parental Advisory program
to alert parents to explicit lyrics in music for young consumers.
Fischer speculates that recent regulations in the Patriot Act initi-
ated by President George W. Bush after the terrorist attacks of
September 11, 2001, could result in censoring popular music that
could be interpreted as "domestic terrorism" or "dangerous to
human life."

In terms of historical time, the two hundred twenty-plus
year history of the United States of America is an instant.
In terms of governance by the rule of law, the effectiveness of
the United States Constitution over a slightly shorter period,
is a modern marvel. In addition to setting up the workings of
a form of representative government, it grants numerous, substantial rights to citizens (initially property owning white
males, now somewhat more egalitarian), protecting and empowering them in their encounters with State power. Fundamental among these rights are those set out in the First
Amendment to the Constitution:

Paul D. Fischer, "What If They Gave a Culture War and Nobody Came?" *Prospects for Free Musical Expression in the United States*, www.freemuse.org, 2001. Reproduced by permission.

Congress shall make no law respecting an establishment of religion, or prohibiting the free exercise thereof; or abridging freedom of speech, or of the press; or the right of the people to peaceably assemble and to petition the government for a redress of grievances.

With regard to freedoms of speech and the press, a landmark case with implications for popular music was settled in 1735. New York newspaperman John Peter Zenger was charged with libel by the British authorities for the content of the *New York Weekly Journal* which he published, but did not write. The case, which Zenger won, is usually discussed in terms of its significance as a departure from British libel law, and a victory for colonial press freedom. In this context, some of the allegedly libelous material must be considered at face value. Part of what Zenger published, were lyrics to ballads lampooning the British colonial governor and his cronies, and he was exonerated. From this point forward, song lyrics were presumptively protected speech in America. If there is any lingering doubt, in a 1985 opinion in the case *Cinevision Corp. v. City of Burbank*, the Court of Appeals for the 9th Circuit plainly stated: "music is a form of expression that is protected by the First Amendment." Even with this protection, the security of music as expression in America is not assured and begs closer scrutiny.

Despite the Constitutional provision that Congress, the legislature, "make no law," the Supreme Court, the nation's highest judicial authority has, over the years, identified three areas of speech that fall outside the First Amendment's protection. These are obscenity, inciteful speech or "fighting words," and speech that could cause harm to minors. Popular music has been challenged in court in all these areas. . . .

Contemporary Laws Restricting Musical Expression

The current era of concern for popular music as expression was touched off in the mid-nineteen-eighties when a Senate subcommittee held Hearings to learn about consumer concerns related to heavy metal music. . . . In 1992, the legislature in the state of Washington passed a content-based regulation. It amended an unenforced 1969 law against sale and distribution of "erotic material" to include "sound recordings." A case was brought on behalf of Washington state based musicians, retailers, national record companies and others, by attorneys for the American Civil Liberties Union (ACLU) of Washington. They argued that the law was unconstitutional because it violated individual rights to speech and due process, that it constituted a prior restraint, and was vague. Four months after the law took effect, King County Superior Court judge declared the law unconstitutional. Judge Mary Brucker's October 29th 1992 opinion stated, "(T)he basic flaw in the statute is the denial of persons affected to know that a sound recording has been determined to be erotic. . . Knowing the possibility exists causes self-censorship which deprives creativity." There are few impediments to legislatures passing unconstitutional laws. It takes the interpretation of a court to prove them so.

Despite the "no law" admonition of the Constitution, federal lawmakers are not immune from the practice either. If the issue "plays well" in the media and at home, especially with the minority of the population most likely to vote, many American elected representatives appear quite willing to let the courts sort out issues of constitutionality. Preferably after the next election cycle. On February 8, 1996 the Communications Decency Act which criminalized transmission of "indecent" and "patently offensive" material over the internet was enacted into law. While not specifically about popular music, it is content-based, and music files are a significant percentage of online content. Led by the ACLU, a suit was filed in federal district court in Philadelphia. After issuing a temporary restraining order barring implementation of the law, a three judge panel found abridgements of the first and fifth amendments in the law and granted a preliminary injunction against it. In his opinion, Judge Stewart Dalzell wrote:

If the goal of our First Amendment jurisprudence is the 'individual dignity and choice' that arises from 'putting the decision as to what views shall be voiced largely into the hands of each of us,' then we should be especially vigilant in preventing content-based regulation of a medium that every minute allows individual citizens to actually make those decisions. Any content-based regulation of the internet, no matter how benign the purpose, could burn the global village to roast the pig.

The Department of Justice appealed to the Supreme Court, which heard the case on March 19th, 1997. On June 26th 1997 the Supreme Court issued a 7-2 decision agreeing with the lower court, the Communications Decency Act was unconstitutional. The law had offered no definition of "indecency," did not require a finding of a lack of "socially redeeming value," and could have a "chilling effect" on speech on the internet. The politicians moved on to the Child Online Protection Act (COPA). Signed into law by President Clinton in October 1998, this law made a narrower attempt at content-based restrictions on the internet, commercial distribution of material deemed "harmful to minors." This language makes specific reference to the judicial precedent that material "harmful to minors" is not protected by the First Amendment. The High Court argued that the State has a compelling interest in the well being of the nation's young people because they are the foundation of its future. As a result, content-based restrictions narrowly tailored to further the government's compelling interest of preventing harm are constitutional. In February of 1999 a federal judge in Philadelphia issued an injunction against enforcement of COPA ruling it unconstitutional on speech grounds. In June of 2000 the 3rd Circuit Court of Appeals affirmed COPA was unconstitutional on different grounds, the impossibility of enforcing "community standards" on the internet. American speech law could have required every internet communication to abide by the most restrictive community's standards. The Department of Justice was granted certiorari [a review of the lower court's decision] by the Supreme Court and the case was argued on November 28th 2001. An 8-1 decision was handed down on May 13th 2002 stating that the lower court should not have invalidated the law based solely on "community standards" but that it could be unconstitutional on other grounds. Additional appeals may be pending.[1]

These recent happenings make it clear that America's Congress, the Senate and House, the legislative branch of the federal government, is actively pursuing content-based restrictions on speech that could include popular music. Thus far, America's courts have provided a substantive check on the wishes of legislators to regulate speech in instances where popular music could be impacted. Another law, which could change all this, must be mentioned here, but the sweeping nature of its language and lack of a record of enforcement attempts under its provisions make discussion of it entirely speculative. This is the USA Patriot Act, "Uniting and Strengthening America by Providing Appropriate Tools Required to Intercept and Obstruct Terrorism," passed in the wake of the attacks of September 11th, 2001. This law could impact politically engaged popular music and artists most drastically. . . .

Obscenity, Fighting Words, and Harm to Minors

Popular music has been challenged in court on the grounds that it has fallen into one of the three areas Supreme Court jurisprudence has left unprotected by the First Amendment, obscenity, inciteful speech (fighting words), or causing harm to minors. Government, however, is not the only source of legal action. In the obscenity case involving music, the artist ini-

---

1. On March 6, 2003, the 3rd Circuit Court again struck down the law as unconstitutional, arguing that it would hinder protected speech among adults. The decision was appealed and in 2004 the Supreme Court heard *Ashcroft v. American Civil Liberties Union* and upheld the block of enforcement, declaring the law unconstitutional once again.

tiated the action. In February of 1990 a Broward County (Florida) Sheriff purchased a copy of *As Nasty As They Wanna Be* by 2Live Crew and transcribed the lyrics of six of its eighteen tracks. He requested a finding of probable cause on obscenity, and in March, Judge Mel Grossman issued an advisory opinion that the material was probably obscene. On that advice, Sheriffs in uniform delivered letters to area record retailers "as a matter of courtesy" that further sales would result in their arrest. The next week, Skyywalker Records filed suit on the question of obscenity and whether the Sheriffs had put an illegal prior restraint on the recording. Judge Jose Gonzalez found both an illegal prior restraint (favoring the band), and obscenity. Judge Gonzalez's obscenity ruling was overturned on appeal, and Florida's appeal to the United States Supreme Court was not granted. The Apellate opinion negating the finding of obscenity prevailed.

In the area of speech that would incite "imminent lawless action," the fighting words doctrine originated in the [1969] case *Brandenburg v. Ohio*, two heavy metal artists were separately brought to court. Based on a 1985 incident, a case was brought in Nevada in 1988 that became known as *Vance v. Judas Priest*. The incident involved a suicide and suicide attempt by two young men while listening to Judas Priest's music. The complainants originally argued for a causal link between listening to the music and taking lawless action (suicide), invoking the fighting words doctrine. They later shifted their causal argument to the presence of "backmasked" messages urging "do it," and it became a product liability case, successfully fought by the band and their record label. The case known as *Waller v. Osbourne*, involving Ozzy Osbourne stayed with the "inciteful speech" argument. It ended when, in 1992, the Supreme Court declined to hear a final appeal of the case. The appellate court had overturned the finding of a causal link between listening and lawless action saying in part, "liability will only attach when the *intention* of dissemination was to cause the ensuing injury." That would mean thousands of suicides. Again, the musical artist prevailed—but not until after years of uncertainty over the possibility of an unfavorable outcome.

In the area of material "harmful to minors," it was the San Francisco punk band Dead Kennedys who were taken to court. It wasn't about the music on the band's third album *Frankenchrist*, it had to do with an enclosed poster by renown fantasy artist H.R. Giger. Despite a warning on the exterior of the package about potentially "shocking, repulsive, offensive" art within, the band was charged with distributing materials harmful to minors. Giger's "Landscape #20: Where Are We Coming From," described in court as showing "nine disembodied genital sex acts of a color and texture resembling armadillo skin" was the cause. It cost the band sixty thousand dollars of their own money to defend. They had no major label assistance, won the case, and broke up. Few cases involving popular music have been brought since these. Obscenity and inciteful speech proved difficult to argue successfully, but the "harm to minors" area of law is open to further probing. That is why this language has been thought viable in legislative proposals. Congress does not just pass laws. They have the power to investigate topics deemed important to their role in governing or that could lead to future legislation.

Legislative Hearings Brought by Citizen Groups

Part of the reason so few content based laws on music and media have been passed by state and federal legislators is the check that the courts have on them by interpreting constitutionality. The limitations in this area have motivated legislators into other courses of action, most notably, Hearings. On September 19th 1985, the senate Subcommittee on Communication of the Commerce, Science and Transportation Committee held a Hearing on so-called "porn rock." A private citizens group, the Parents Music Resource Center (PMRC) was calling for an extensive content based labeling system for sound recordings. PMRC membership included the wives of ten Senators, six Representatives, and a few Bush administration figures. Music artists Frank Zappa, John Denver, and Dee Snider of Twisted Sister testified against product labeling. While the Subcommittee took no action on the proposal, the media attention gained by the PMRC during the Hearings, led to private negotiations with Recording Industry Association of America (RIAA) on behalf of its member record labels. On November first of that year the RIAA announced an agreement that its members would voluntarily put a sticker reading "Parental Advisory: Explicit Lyrics" on the exterior of the package. Because the labeling program was voluntary and not the result of *government* action, it is technically not censorship, but the public attention afforded the matter by the Hearings on Capitol Hill may have put pressure on the RIAA to settle.

Hearings were held on both sides of the Congressional aisle in 1994, catalyzed by another citizens group, the National Political Congress of Black Women (NPCBW). On February 11th and May 5th the House Subcommittee on Commerce, Consumer Protection and Competitiveness held Hearings on "gangsta rap." On February 23rd, the Senate Subcommittee on Juvenile Justice did the same. The legislators who convened both sets of Hearings went to great pains explaining that no legislation was being contemplated, but that information was being gathered. They heard from a broad range of witnesses that included record label executives, law enforcement, youth services, and even a rapper. They heard NPCBW President C. Delores Tucker call this music "obscene," and "injecting poison into the veins of the nation's future." These Hearings did not achieve as high a media profile as those in 1985, but it did position the NPCBW and Dr. Tucker well for future actions against the private corporations bringing these products to market. While the Subcommittee took no direct action on the issue, they assisted in giving visibility and added credibility to another opponent of music as expression.

Legislative Hearings Brought by Legislators

A somewhat different set of Hearings were convened in November of 1997. The Senate Government Affairs Subcommittee heard testimony on the topic, "The Impact Of Popular Music On Youth." A key difference is that his Hearing was called by two members of the Subcommittee itself, Senator Sam Brownback, Republican of Kansas and Senator Joe Lieberman, Democrat of Connecticut. Lieberman, it should be noted, was the Vice President candidate in Al Gore's unsuccessful Presidential campaign in 2000. Lieberman is considered a viable candidate for the Democratic Presidential nomination in 2004.[2] Both Senators spoke as the Hearings began, Brownback as convener of the session and Lieberman as a witness, making certain the intent behind the Hearings and the concerns of both Senators were made public. Brownback, acknowledging it is a minority of popular music, expressed concern about songs glorifying violence, racism, murder, mayhem, and the abuse of women, saying:

> It stands to reason that prolonged exposure to such hate filled lyrics during the formative teen years could have an impact on one's attitude and assumptions and thus decisions and behavior. Understanding the nature and extent of the influence of music violence may well be the first step towards better addressing the problems and pathologies besetting our youth.

Lieberman's statement also acknowledged that only some music is problematic, but focused his ire on the companies of the "mostly a very constructive, elevating industry" who release these products.

2. Senator Lieberman campaigned for the Democratic presidential nomination in 2004, but dropped out of the race after gaining little support from primary voters.

The men and women who run the large corporations who turn out this music must stop hiding behind the first amendment and confront the damage that some, and I emphasize some, of their products are doing. We're not talking censorship here, but citizenship.

Brownback confidently made the cause and effect connection between music listening and action that was impossible to prove in the courtroom, and without hearing testimony from a single social scientist. Rather than work from a case-by-case examination of music alleged to be having such impacts, Brownback would have the whole industry publicly defend its practices. Lieberman's appeal is purely corporate, taking aim at the sense of social responsibility to the mainstream that those wielding corporate power are expected to have. Perhaps acknowledging the lack of progress in court-based attempts at content-based regulation of culture, Senator Lieberman called upon the executives in the industry to "police themselves" as other culture industries (e.g., film, television) had in the past. He emphasizes that his notion of corporate citizenship involves a cessation of First Amendment based protestations and acceptance that damage has been done by some of their products. He suggests that a proper response might include behaviors restricted from government itself, limiting some musical expression for "marketplace reasons," loyalty to mainstream stability, not censorship. No competent industry executive would openly accept such a notion of product liability, but some were vulnerable to criticism in their role as "corporate citizens."

Linking Music to School Violence

Also different about this Hearing was a much shorter witness list, with only Hilary Rosen of the RIAA speaking from an even vaguely pro-music position. Seemingly oblivious to the court cases already settled in this area, the testimony centered on a Mr. Kuntz who argued for a causal link between his son's suicide and listening to a (stickered) Marilyn Manson CD. Another set of Hearings built on this model were held in July of 1998 with the title "Labels and Lyrics: Do Parental Advisory Stickers Inform Consumers and Parents?" Senators Brownback and Lieberman catalyzed these Hearings in front of The Senate Commerce, Science and Transportation Committee, a step up organizationally from the PMRC days. Again there was a short witness list, centering on a teacher from Jonesboro, Arkansas who testified on the causal link she believed existed between listening to "gangsta rap" and firing on classmates at their school. Toward the end of the Hearing Senator Brownback promised that they were "far from done" with this issue.

In the spring of 1999 a student led attack with multiple fatalities occurred at Columbine High School in Littleton, Colorado. The musical tastes of the shooters quickly became a matter of public discussion and Marilyn Manson was quickly scapegoated for their actions. Legislators responded with a flurry of proposals they hoped could deal with the perceived crisis with popular culture. Senator Lieberman with Republican Senator John McCain of Arizona proposed the "21st Century Media Responsibility Act of 1999" which would have created ratings for popular materials on an intensity of violence scale. Senator Henry Hyde of Illinois added an amendment to a Crime Bill that would have banned the sale or rental of warning labeled material to minors (under 17) and required retailers to provide access to the lyrics of all songs on sale. Senator Brownback proposed a "Committee On American Culture," that would have been empowered to ferret out the sources of "cultural regression," and seek strategies for "cultural renewal." None of these proposals became law, but give evidence to a range of strategies for legislating aspects of culture that are in the minds of those in office in Washington, D.C. Following a Presidentially mandated report by the Federal Trade Commission on the marketing of inappropriate products to youth, Hearings were held about movies, popular music and computer games. This session centered on frequency and intensity of violence, the possibility of a rating system for all these media with specific age guidelines, and improper venues for advertising of products with violent content. Warnings were voiced to the industries, but again, no action was taken.

That is the extent of the federal record of discussions that bear specifically on popular music. It doesn't begin to detail activity in the fifty state legislatures. That is where the most dangerous legislative proposals specifically impacting popular music have been made in recent years. In 1989 Pennsylvania and Missouri considered mandatory record labeling laws and model legislation was circulated nationally in case it passed there. The 1992 Washington "erotic music" law discussed above was next. In 1998 Michigan looked at a concert-rating bill based on whether the concert artist's recorded product had been warning labeled in the previous five years. That would have required warning labels in concert ads. A bill was also proposed that would have allowed local authorities in towns with concert venues to declare some events "harmful to minors." Also in 1998 a bill reached the floor in the Georgia state legislature, which borrowed language from the failed federal proposal to criminalize sale or rental of warning labeled product to minors. A similar bill was proposed, but never got out of committee in Tennessee that year. This front has been fairly quiet for several years but begs constant vigilance.

Regulation Attempts from the Executive Branch

There hasn't been much cause to examine the executive record on popular music, because it rarely goes beyond the level of popular culture bashing campaign rhetoric and Bill Clinton playing the saxophone. However, with the passage of the USA Patriot Act mentioned above, the United States' third branch of government has taken actions which could directly impact popular music as expression in this country. Passed by Congress on October 25th 2001 and signed into law by President George W. Bush the next day, this rapidly developed, 342-page bill couched in patriotic language, consolidated vast new powers with the Executive Branch. The vote in the House of Representatives was 357-66, the Senate's was 98-1, with only Russell Feingold, Democrat of Wisconsin opposed. He said, in part, "I have concluded that this bill does not strike the right balance between empowering law enforcement and protecting civil liberties." The provisions of the new law, primarily intended to counter terrorist activity on United States' soil and beyond, is also in force in many simple criminal cases as well. Among other things, this law lowers standards for government requested surveillance of domestic individuals and removes court oversight from many Executive Branch actions when opposition to or suppression of terrorism is even part of the declared motive. In USA Patriot, the language is often broad to the point of vagueness, and the Bush administration has made it clear they hope the judiciary, when it does have oversight, will interpret it broadly. Some of the law's provisions have sunset clauses, but most will remain in effect until explicitly repealed. This law has the potential for great negative impact on freedom of expression, depending on how it is enforced and implemented.

Limiting discussion here to aspects of USA Patriot that could impact popular music, one must begin with Section 802 that creates a federal crime known as "domestic terrorism," which covers "acts dangerous to human life that are a violation of the criminal laws" if they "appear to be intended . . . to influence the policy of a government by intimidation or coercion," and if they "Occur primarily within the territorial jurisdiction of the United States." This can be construed to include public demonstrations and acts of civil disobedience, even nonviolent ones that protest against and seek to change government policies. Legal dissent. A march or rally, even with all required permits, with aggressive policing and crowd control, could precipitate behaviors that could create "dangers to human life" completely beyond the control of event organizers, raising the possibility of penalties applied under USA Patriot. It is not hard to see that environmental, anti-globalization, or pro- and anti-abortion protesters could soon be labeled "domestic terrorists." What of musicians who perform at rallies that develop crowd control problems? The language of the Act considers "terrorist activities" to include soliciting membership, soliciting funds, or providing material support for any group declared "terrorist" by the government. If the musicians make statements supportive of the organization's aims or urge crowds to make donations in addition to the drawing power of their appearance, they could be individually prosecuted as domestic terrorists. Just by appearing they are providing a form of "material support" to the sponsoring organization, as would any cash donations. Also, the Executive Branch is not required to publicly list the organizations it considers "terrorist." Even tangential association with such a group could open musical artists up to increased surveillance of their telephone, e-mail, and internet traffic, as well as unannounced "sneak and peek" searches of their homes and offices. Such consequences could clearly lead to chilling effects on political speech by musicians and others. If they happen to be non-citizens, the consequences can be even more dire.

Section 411 of USA Patriot would disallow entry into the United States of non-citizens who have used their "position of prominence in any country to endorse or espouse terrorist activity," if the Secretary of State determines that their speech "undermines U.S. efforts to reduce or eliminate terrorist activities." Similar consequences attach if the non-citizen is a representative of a political or social group that is viewed similarly by the Secretary of State. Section 412 vastly expands the Attorney General's power to detain and/or remove non-citizens who are even suspected of falling into the class of "terrorist" while in the country. This can include detention without charges. An ACLU statement [by Laura Murphy] makes clear, "the so-called USA Patriot Act contains a large number of provisions that essentially destroy the check placed by the courts on summary executive action." Even the libertarian Cato Institute has published a paper [titled "The USA Patriot Act: We Deserve Better" by Robert A. Levy] expecting that at some point the Supreme Court "may have to clarify how the civil liberties/national security tradeoff will unfold (Levy, 5). Watch out Chuck D., Bono, Zach, Sting, Ice-T, Peter, Bruce, and other musicians whose work has a political dimension and are known for their activism. The landscape here is very different now. How frequently and aggressively these new laws will be used at all, let alone with impact on popular music, remains to be seen.

Chronology

1734

Journalist and printer John Peter Zenger is acquitted of "seditious libels" against New York Governor William Cosby, increasing the freedom of the press in the American colonies.

1798

During the administration of President John Adams, Congress passes the Alien and Sedition Acts, making it illegal to "write, print, utter, or publish" anything critical of the president or Congress.

1873

Anti-vice crusader Anthony Comstock ushers the Comstock Act through Congress, which bans obscene materials from being sent through the U.S. mails.

1915

The Supreme Court rules in *Mutual Film Corporation v. Industrial Commission of Ohio* that films are exempt from First Amendment protections, giving state censorship boards the power to prevent films from being shown in theaters.

1921

New York State enacts a law that requires the publishers of film newsreels to submit all of their newsreels to the state film censor for approval before showing them to audiences at movie theaters; many other states quickly follow suit.

1922

The Motion Picture Producers and Distributors (later know as the Motion Picture Association of America) begins to enforce the Production Code, which requires Hollywood filmmakers to follow rigid guidelines when producing movies; the Production Code closely regulated filmmaking in the United States for almost fifty years.

1934

The Federal Communications Commission begins to enforce the Federal Communications Act, which requires the media to give equal time to rival political candidates and equal coverage to all sides of a political issue.

1938

The House Committee on Un-American Activities (HUAC) is established in the House of Representatives to root out communism in the United States in the name of national security.

1939

The American Library Association adopts the Library Bill of Rights, which states that the selection of library materials should not be influenced by the politics, race, religion, or nationality of the writer.

1941

After Japan's attack on Pearl Harbor, President Roosevelt empowers an office of censorship to encourage the voluntary self-censorship of the media; the administration's Code of Wartime Practices for the U.S. Press specifies that nothing should be published that might help the enemy war effort.

1951

Under the pressure of the Catholic Church and citizen groups, the Board of Regents of New York declares the Italian film *The Miracle* "sacrilegious" and bans it from movie theaters.

1952

The Supreme Court declares that film distributor Joseph Burstyn cannot be prevented by state film censors from showing the controversial Italian film *The Miracle* in movie theaters; overturning the earlier decision in *Mutual Film Corporation v. Industrial Commission of Ohio*, the court rules that film is a protected form of expression under the First Amendment.

1953

Senator Joseph McCarthy becomes chair of the Senate Permanent Subcommittee on Investigations and calls over 653 witnesses in little over a year to testify about Communist infiltration in the United States.

1954

The Comics Magazine Association of America (CMAA) establishes the Comics Code Authority (CCA) to regulate the content of comic books in the United States.

1966

Congress passes the Freedom of Information Act, making a wide array of government information, including records held by law enforcement agencies, available to the general public.

1968

The Hollywood film industry stops using the Production Code of the Motion Picture Association of America to regulate filmmaking and instead adopts the Classification and Rating Administration (CARA) system that is still in use today, assigning films designations such as X, R, PG, and G.

1969

The decision in the Supreme Court case *Tinker v. Des Moines* rules that the First Amendment protects the freedom of expression of public school students.

1971

The Department of Defense's top secret Pentagon Papers are leaked to the *New York Times*, causing the administration of President Richard Nixon to attempt unsuccessfully to censor their publication.

1973

The Supreme Court in *Miller v. California* reiterates that obscenity is not protected by the First Amendment and establishes the Miller test to determine what constitutes obscenity; most notably, the Miller test established that "community standards" rather than national standards will rule whether material appeals to prurient interest.

1978

The "Whistleblowers" Act, formally listed as the Civil Service Reform Act, protects civil servants who reveal government misconduct from being punished or harassed.

1982

In *New York v. Ferber*, Supreme Court justices rule that the possession or distribution of child pornography is prohibited by law.

1989

One hundred members of Congress denounce the National Endowment for the Arts (NEA) for using federal funds to support an art exhibit that included sexually explicit images; under extreme pressure, the NEA becomes very cautious about granting funds to controversial artists; in *Texas v. Johnson*, the Supreme Court affirms that burning the American flag is a form of expression and therefore is protected by the First Amendment of the Constitution; in reaction, Congress passes the Flag Desecration Act of 1989 to impose criminal penalties against anyone who knowingly desecrates the flag.

1996

Congress passes the Communications Decency Act, criminalizing the transmission of indecent or obscene material over the Internet.

1997

In *Reno v. American Civil Liberties Union*, the Supreme Court rules that the indecency provisions in the Communications Decency Act are unconstitutional.

1998

Congress passes the Child Online Protection Act (COPA) to protect children from harmful sexual material on the Internet; the act is immediately challenged in court and overturned.

2000

Congress passes the Children's Internet Protection Act (CIPA) to limit children's exposure to pornography and other controversial material on the Internet; CIPA is also challenged in court, but the Supreme Court upholds the law as constitutional in 2004.

2001

After the terrorist attacks of September 11, Congress passes the Patriot Act, which relaxes many restrictions on law enforcement agencies to investigate possible terrorist activity; critics of the legislation claim that it unnecessarily compromises freedom of speech and the right to privacy.

Organizations to Contact

American Civil Liberties Union (ACLU)
125 Broad St., 18th Fl., New York, NY 10004
(212) 549-2500 • fax: (212) 549-2646
e-mail: aclu@aclu.org
Web site: www.aclu.org

The ACLU is a national organization that defends Americans' civil rights guaranteed in the U.S. Constitution. It adamantly opposes regulation of all forms of speech, including pornography and hate speech. The ACLU offers numerous reports, fact sheets, and policy statements on a wide variety of issues. Publications include the briefing papers "Freedom of Expression" and "Hate Speech on Campus" and the report "Freedom Under Fire: Dissent in Post-9/11 America."

American Library Association (ALA)
50 E. Huron St., Chicago, IL 60611
(800) 545-2433 • fax: (312) 440-9374
e-mail: ala@ala.org
Web site: www.ala.org

The ALA is the nation's primary professional organization for librarians. Through its Office for Intellectual Freedom (OIF), the ALA supports free access to libraries and library materials. The OIF also monitors and opposes efforts to ban books. The ALA's sister organization, the Freedom to Read Foundation, provides legal defense for libraries. Publications include the bimonthly *Newsletter on Intellectual Freedom*, articles, fact sheets, and policy statements, including "Freedom to Read Statement," "Freedom to View Statement," and "Resolution Reaffirming the Principles of Intellectual Freedom in the Aftermath of Terrorist Attacks."

Canadian Association for Free Expression (CAFE)
PO Box 332, Station B
Etobicoke, ON M9W 5L3   Canada
(905) 897-7221 • fax: (905) 277-3914
e-mail: cafe@canadafirst.net
Web site: www.canadianfreespeech.com

CAFE, one of Canada's leading civil liberties groups, works to strengthen the freedom of speech and freedom of expression provisions in the Canadian Charter of Rights and Freedoms. It lobbies politicians and researches threats to freedom of speech. Publications include specialized reports, leaflets, and the *Free Speech Monitor*, which is published ten times per year.

Cato Institute
1000 Massachusetts Ave. NW, Washington, DC   20001-5403
(202) 842-0200 • fax: (202) 842-3490
e-mail: cato@cato.org
Web site: www.cato.org

The Cato Institute is a libertarian public policy research foundation. It advocates limited government and strongly opposes regulations on speech. The institute distributes books, policy papers, reports, and the triannual *Cato Journal*.

Concerned Women for America (CWA)
1015 Fifteenth St. NW, Suite 1100, Washington, DC   20005
(202) 488-7000 • fax: (202) 448-0806
e-mail: mail@cwfa.org
Web site: www.cwfa.org

CWA promotes conservative values and is concerned with creating an environment that is conducive to building strong families and raising healthy children. The organization advocates the use of Interact filters in schools and libraries and supports the passage of the Children's Internet Protection Act to block material that may be harmful to minors. CWA publishes the bimonthly *Family Voice* and numerous press releases and reports, including "Hard-Core Harm: Why You Can't Be Soft on Porn."

Electronic Frontier Foundation (EFF)
454 Shotwell St., San Francisco, CA   94110
(415) 436-9333 • fax: (415) 436-9993
e-mail: ask@eff.org
Web site: www.eff.org

EFF works to protect privacy and freedom of expression in the arena of computers and the Internet. Its missions include supporting litigation that protects First Amendment rights. EFF's Web site publishes an electronic bulletin, *Effector*, and the guidebook *Protecting Yourself Online: The Definitive Resource on Safety, Freedom, and Privacy in Cyberspace.*

Family Research Council (FRC)
801 G St. NW, Washington, DC   20001
(202) 393-2100 • fax: (202) 393-2134
e-mail: corrdept@frc.org
Web site: www.frc.org

The Family Research Council is an organization that believes pornography degrades women and children. The FRC seeks to strengthen current obscenity laws. It publishes the monthly newsletter *Washington Watch* and the bimonthly journal *Family Policy*, which features a full-length essay in each issue, such as "Keeping Libraries User and Family Friendly: The Challenge of Internet Pornography." The FRC also publishes policy papers, including "Indecent Proposal: The NEA Since the Supreme Court Decency Decision" and "Internet Filtering and Blocking Technology."

Free Speech Coalition
PO Box 10480, Canoga Park, CA   91309
(800) 845-8503 • fax: (818) 886-5914
e-mail: freespeech@freespeechcoalition.com
Web site: www.freespeechcoalition.com

The Free Speech Coalition is a trade association that represents members of the adult entertainment industry. It seeks to protect the industry from attempts to censor pornography. Publications include fact sheets, *Free Speech X-Press*, and the report "The Truth About the Adult Entertainment Industry."

Freedom Forum
1101 Wilson Blvd., Arlington, VA   22209
(703) 528-0800 • fax: (703) 284-3770
e-mail: news@freedomforum.org
Web site: www.freedomforum.org

The Freedom Forum is a national organization that works to protect free speech and freedom of the press. It monitors developments in media and First Amendment issues on its Web site. The forum's First Amendment Center focuses on the study and exploration of free-expression issues. It publishes the annual report "State of the First Amendment," the teacher's guide *Free Speech and Music*, the report "Violence and the Media: An Exploration of Cause, Effect, and the First Amendment," and other studies and briefing papers.

The Heritage Foundation
214 Massachusetts Ave. NE, Washington, DC   20002-4999
(800) 544-4843 • fax: (202) 546-8328
e-mail: info@heritage.org
Web site: www.heritage.org

The foundation is a conservative public policy organization dedicated to individual liberty, free-market principles, and limited government. It favors limiting freedom of the press when that freedom threatens national security. Its resident scholars publish position papers on a wide range of issues through publications such as the weekly *Backgrounder* and the bimonthly *Policy Review*.

Morality in Media (MIM)
475 Riverside Dr., Suite 239, New York, NY   10115
(212) 870-3222 • fax: (212) 870-2765
e-mail: mim@moralityinmedia.org
Web site: www.moralityinmedia.org

Morality in Media is an interfaith organization that fights pornography and opposes indecency in the mainstream media. It maintains the National Obscenity Law Center, a clearinghouse of legal materials on obscenity law. MIM publishes the bimonthlies *Morality in Media* and *Obscenity Law Bulletin* and several reports, including "Pornography's Effects on Adults and Children" and "Minors' Access to Pornography on the Internet Through Library and School Computers."

National Coalition Against Censorship (NCAC)
275 Seventh Ave., New York, NY   10001
(212) 807-6222 • fax: (212) 807-6245
e-mail: ncac@ncac.org
Web site: www.ncac.org

The coalition represents more than forty national organizations that work to prevent suppression of free speech and the press. NCAC educates the public about the dangers of censorship and how to oppose it. The coalition publishes the quarterly *Censorship News*, articles, various reports, and background papers. Papers include "Censorship's Tools Du Jour: V-Chips, TV Ratings, PICS, and Internet Filters" and "Free Speech in Wartime."

National Congress of Black Women (NCBW)
8484 Georgia Ave., Suite 420, Silver Spring, MD   20910
(877) 274-1198 • fax: (301) 562-8303
e-mail: info@npcbw.org
Web site: www.npcbw.org

The NCBW supports the advancement of African American women in politics and government. The congress also engages in research on critical issues that affect the quality of life of African American women and youth. Through its Commission on Entertainment, the NCBW campaigns against the glorification of violence, misogyny, pornography, and drugs in popular entertainment. It publishes project reports on its Web site, including "Crusading Against Gangsta/Porno Rap."

People for the American Way (PFAW)
2000 M St. NW, Suite 400, Washington, DC   20036
(800) 326-7329 • fax: (202) 293-2672

e-mail: pfaw@pfaw.org
Web site: www.pfaw.org

PFAW works to promote citizen participation in democracy and safeguard the principles of the U.S. Constitution, including the right to free speech. It publishes a variety of fact sheets, articles, and position statements on its Web site and distributes the e-mail newsletter *Freedom to Learn Online.*

For Further Reading

Books

Randall P. Bezanson, *Speech Stories: How Free Can Speech Be?* New York: New York University Press, 1998.

Robert H. Bork, *Slouching Towards Gomorrah: Modern Liberalism and American Decline*. New York: Regan, 1996.

Ellen Henson Brinkley, *Caught Off Guard: Teachers Rethinking Censorship and Controversy*. Boston: Allyn and Bacon, 1999.

Tammy Bruce, *The New Thought Police: Inside the Left's Assault on Free Speech and Free Minds*. Roseville, CA: Forum, 2001.

Francis G. Couvares, ed., *Movie Censorship and American Culture*. Washington, DC: Smithsonian Institution, 1996.

Richard Delgado and Jean Stefancic, *Must We Defend Nazis? Hate Speech, Pornography, and the New First Amendment*. New York: New York University Press, 1997.

June Edwards, *Opposing Censorship in the Public Schools: Religion, Morality, and Literature*. Mahwah, NJ: Lawrence Erlbaum, 1998.

Jonathan Green, ed., *The Encyclopedia of Censorship*. New York: Facts On File, 2005.

Marjorie Heins, *Not in Front of the Children: "Indecency," Censorship, and the Innocence of Youth*. New York: Hill and Wang, 2001.

Nat Hentoff, *Free Speech for Me—but Not for Thee: How the American Left and Right Relentlessly Censor Each Other*. New York: HarperCollins, 1992.

Nicholas J. Karolides, ed., *Censored Books II: Critical Viewpoints, 1985–2000*. Lanham, MD: Scarecrow, 2002.

Sheila Suess Kennedy, ed., *Free Expression in America: A Documentary History*. Westport, CT: Greenwood, 1999.

Kathryn Kolbert and Zak Mettger, *Censoring the Web*. New York: New Press, 2001.

David Lowenthal, *No Liberty for License: The Forgotten Logic of the First Amendment*. Dallas: Spence, 1997.

Charles Lyons, *The New Censors: Movies and the Culture Wars*. Philadelphia: Temple University Press, 1997.

Eric Nuzum, *Parental Advisory: Music Censorship in America*. New York: Perennial, 2001.

Robert S. Peck, *Libraries, the First Amendment, and Cyberspace: What You Need to Know*. Chicago: American Library Association, 2000.

Peter Phillips, *Censored 2005: The Top 25 Censored Stories*. New York: Seven Stories, 2004.

Annie J. Randall, ed., *Music, Power, and Politics*. New York: Routledge, 2005.

Diane Ravitch, *The Language Police: How Pressure Groups Restrict What Students Learn*. New York: Vintage, 2004.

Louise S. Robbins, *Censorship and the American Library: The American Library Association's Response to Threats to Intellectual Freedom, 1939–1969*. Westport, CT: Greenwood, 1996.

Timothy C. Shiell, *Campus Hate Speech on Trial*. Lawrence: University Press of Kansas, 1998.

John S. Simmons and Eliza T. Dresang, *School Censorship in the 21st Century: A Guide for Teachers and School Library Media Specialists*. Newark, DE: International Reading Association, 2001.

Sarah J. Smith, *Children, Cinema, and Censorship: From Dracula to the Dead End Kids.* New York: I.B. Tauris, 2005.

Ann K. Symons and Sally Gardner Reed, eds., *Speaking Out! Voices in Celebration of Intellectual Freedom.* Chicago: American Library Association, 1999.

Jonathan Wallace and Mark Mangan, *Sex, Laws, and Cyberspace: Freedom and Censorship on the Frontiers of the Online Revolution.* New York: Henry Holt, 1997.

Periodicals

Andrew Brown, "The Limits of Freedom," *New Statesman,* February 12, 1999.

Conscience, "Index: A Selective Timeline of Censorship, 1235–2003," Spring 2003. Available from 1436 U St. NW, Suite 301, Washington, DC 20009-3997.

Michael Cromartie, "Give Me Liberty, but Don't Give Me Filth," *Christianity Today,* May 19, 1997.

Emily Eakin, "The Censor and the Artists: A Murky Border," *New York Times,* November 26, 2002.

Economist, "Banned Music," November 28, 1998.

Stephen Goode, "Censorship on College Campuses," *Insight on the News,* June 3, 2002. Available from 3600 New York Ave. NE, Washington, DC 20002.

Linda Greenhouse, "Sides Debate Web Access in Libraries," *New York Times,* March 6, 2003.

Irving Kristol, "Liberal Censorship and the Common Culture," *Society,* September–October 1999.

David Lowenthal, "The Case for Censorship," *Weekly Standard,* August 23, 1999. Available from 1150 Seventeenth St. NW, Suite 505, Washington, DC 20036-4617.

Jay Nordlinger, "Getting Aroused: What It Takes to Combat Porn," *National Review*, November 19, 2001.

Sara Paretsky, "The New Censorship," *New Statesman*, June 2, 2003.

Post Standard, "Filtering Freedom—Law Limiting Library Internet Use Reaches Too Far," July 11, 2006.

Anna Quindlen, "With a No. 2 Pencil, Delete: The Destruction of Literature in the Name of Children," *Newsweek*, June 17, 2002.

Roxana Robinson, "Censorship or Common Sense?" *New York Times*, October 19, 1998.

Brian Siano, "Tales from the Crypt," *Humanist*, March–April 1994.

Max J. Skidmore, "Censorship: Who Needs It? How the Conventional Wisdom Restricts Information's Free Flow," *Journal of Popular Culture*, Winter 2001.

Patrick J. Sloyan, "This Is War: Hiding Bodies: How the White House Makes Sure That Members of the Press Don't End Up Showing You Anything Too Upsetting," *Rolling Stone*, March 20, 2003.

Stuart Taylor Jr., "How Campus Censors Squelch Freedom of Speech," *National Journal*, July 12, 2003. Available from 1501 M St. NW, #300, Washington, DC 20005.

Jesse Walker, "Intolerant Alliance: Censors of Right and Left Have Been Cooperating for Years," *Reason*, March 2001.

Bernard A. Weisberger, "Chasing Smut in Every Medium," *American Heritage*, December 1997.

Jonathan Yardley, "Read No Evil: A Textbook Case of Censorship," *Washington Post*, June 12, 2003.

Charles M. Young, "Censure and Censorship," *Billboard*, November 1, 1994. Available from 770 Broadway, New York, NY 10003.

Videos/DVDs

Hollywood Censored. Directed by David Espar. Public Broadcasting Service, 2000.

Patently Offensive: Porn Under Siege. Directed by Blair Gershkow and Harriet Koskoff. Filmmakers Library, 1991.

Smothered: The Censorship Struggles of the Smothers Brothers Comedy Hour. Directed by Maureen Muldaur. New Video Group, 2002.

Index

classified information, 55
  see also national security
Clinton, Bill, 100, 140, 219, 227
CNN (Cable News Network), 101–102
Code of Wartime Practices, 104–105
Coe, Frank, 71
Cold War era, 49–96, 144
  see also censorship methods; McCarthyism
colonial American era, 20–35
Columbine High School violence, 226
comic books, 14–15, 51–52
Comics Code Authority (CCA), 14–15, 52
Committee of Catholics for Cultural Action, 93
"Committee on American Culture," 226–27
Committee on Public Information (CPI), 104, 113
Commonweal magazine, 92
Communications Decency Act, 207, 218–20
communism. *See* Cold War era; McCarthyism
Communist Party, USA, 54, 58
  see also blacklisting; Cold War era; McCarthyism
Compromised Campus: The Collaboration of Universities with the Intelligence Community, The (Desmond), 57
"compulsory patriotism," 182–83
Comstock, Anthony, 19, 36–44, 45
Comstock laws, 19
  argument against, 45–48
  argument for, 36–44
"Condemnation of the Party Press" (newspaper article), 28–29

conscientious objectors (COs), 124
contemporary/modern culture, 173–230
Cooney, John, 93
Copeland, David A., 20–35
Corallo, Mark, 160
Cosby, William, 22, 26
countercultural movement of 1960s and 1970s, 174
  see also New Left
counterintelligence. *See* CIA (Central Intelligence Agency); FBI (Federal Bureau of Investigation)
"credibility gap," 105–106
Creel, George, 115
Crowther, Bosley, 95
Cuban missile crisis, 144
Cushman, Robert E., 116
Cyberpatrol, 197, 198

Dalzell, Stewart, 218–19
"Dangers of Papers and Pamphlets, The," 26–27
Dellums, Ron, 139
DeMille, Cecil B., 87
Denney, Len, 179
Desmond, Sigmund, 57
Dimick, Barbara, 199
Dineen, Fitzgeorge, 88
Disney, Walt, 86
"Disruption of the New Left" (FBI program), 58–59
Domestic Security Enhancement Act of 2003, 161–62
Douglas, William O., 94, 163, 215
Drechsel, Robert, 202
Dulles, John Foster, 72

early 20th century, 19, 36–44, 45–48
Easley, Ralph, 114